WEEDING THE GARDEN OF EDEN

Mary —
You were there for some of these stories. Enjoy,

WEEDING THE GARDEN OF EDEN

A Memoir

David

**by
DAVID SEVERE**

MILL CITY PRESS

Mill City Press, Inc.
2301 Lucien Way #415
Maitland, FL 32751
407.339.4217
www.millcitypress.net

© 2018 by David Severe

All rights reserved. No part of this publication may be reproduced, stored in a retrieval system, or transmitted, in any form or by any means, electronic, mechanical, photocopying, recording, or otherwise, without the prior written permission of the author.

Printed in the United States of America

ISBN-13: 978-1-54565-009-7

~~ For ~~

Paula, precious life companion,
Sherri and Art, children of blessings,

Christine, Taylor, Mark, David Evan,
grandchildren of brilliance,

And eight wonderful great grandchildren:
Madison, Jack, Manakai, Sam,
Emily, Azlan, Macie and Rumi.

With special thanks to
Carolyn Wall, teacher extraordinaire,
and The Dead Writers Society,
companions in search of a "Done Stamp."

With special appreciation to the
Mission Council of the South Central Jurisdiction
of The United Methodist Church
And to Art Severe for the design of the cover art

A PARABLE

Adam's days were filled with fishing, hunting and gathering fruit. Other than that, he lolled under an olive tree and tossed pebbles in the stream.

Eve fussed about their cave and gathered things with which to "*décor*." She arranged stones of various colors leading up to the entryway. She said, "we must make the place inviting."

Adam wondered *for whom*, but didn't ask.

She fetched a plant from near the great falls. "Adam, set this flower in the ground next to my rocks, and water it, please."

Adam thought, *what's a flower?* But he was compliant.

Daily she returned with more specimens and told Adam where to dig holes and plant them– until Eve's garden flowered on both sides of the path from the cave to the stream.

One day she said, "Adam, prickly things have grown among my flowers. Pull them up."

Adam looked puzzled. "What are you talking about?"

Pointing out the coiling briars, she said, "Those . . . those . . . *weeds*."

So it came to pass that Adam was down on his hands and knees, tugging at weeds, when the Lord strolled by.

"Evenin', Adam."

"Evenin' Lord."

"What are you doing?"

"Sir, Eve said I should pull up these weeds."

And the Lord said, ". . . *Weeds?"*

> *And God saw everything he had made, and behold, it was very good.*
> Genesis 1:31

NATIVE SOIL – NATIVE SON

RICH BLACK SOIL EXTENDS SOME FIFTY MILES south from the Kansas line into the rolling hills of northern Oklahoma. Gradually it gives way to the red earth for which my home state is known. That change appears near Perry, the seat of Noble County. Here I was brought as an infant and lived until I went off to college.

Wheat, oil, cattle and kids flourished, and businesses thrived in the 1940s and 50s. Black locust trees dotted the city, and each spring their sweet, almost sickening aroma penetrated the town. Streets running north and south were numbered, while those running east and west were named alphabetically after trees – Ash, Birch, Cedar, Elm, Fir and Locust. I grew up on Fir. Apparently, the town fathers couldn't think of a tree starting with D, so named that street Delaware.

The opening of the Cherokee Strip at high noon on September 16, 1889, brought settlers from all directions in what was the greatest land giveaway in history. The *strip*, thirty-five miles wide and 165 miles long, was part of the Cherokee Outlet. U.S. Marshalls and civil engineers platted townships. Perry, in the Auburn Township, was on the eastern edge of that run – laid out with a courthouse in the center of a town square.

When we got engaged, Paula and I went to B. C. Clark's jewelry store in Oklahoma City, to buy our rings. Mr. Clark, the store's founder, learned I was from Perry, and told us that he almost started his business there. The day the Cherokee Strip opened he rode the train from Kansas, and when it stopped in Perry, he jumped off – ran down the street and staked claims in two places. He then looked at the map and discovered he had put one marker in the middle of an intersection, and the other on designated school land. Retrieving his claims, he boarded the train and continued to Oklahoma City.

By the time I was born, forty-five years after the run, two other structures sat on the block with the courthouse – the Carnegie Library and the United States Post Office. Every store around the square was occupied. There were two movie theaters, two five and dimes, three department stores, three pharmacies, three banks, the Kumback Lunch, my uncle Forest's Severe's Café, a pool hall, and Moe's Beer and Sandwich parlor. Each morning the 7 a.m. whistle at the electric plant signaled the beginning of the work day and at 6 p.m. sent the laborers home.

Perry was a great place to grow up. I roamed free and tested the edges of selfhood. Almost everyone knew me – a handicap if I tried to get away with anything. Life revolved around school, family and church. I was cared for, protected and, although I didn't realize it, prepared to seek a world beyond the Noble county line.

IT'S SPRING AND THE LOCUSTS ARE IN BLOOM

Black locust trees spread across my hometown
Gnarled bark, as dark as midnight
Branches armed with foreboding thorns

No street or neighborhood was without them
But if one wondered why they weren't cut down
Any warm spring day would tell you why

Blooms emerged from those thorny limbs
Draped like clusters of translucent grapes
And the perfusion of the sweetest aroma

A heady, invasive city-wide happening
The whole town annually enrapt by their spell
In a week or so they'd earned their keep

Now they are almost all gone, felled, or diseased
And hardly anyone left can remember them at all
But they are in my memory forever.

THE BEST SHOW IN TOWN

SUMMERS WERE EXCITING IN MY CHILDHOOD. No school, plenty of play time. The pace was slow. Television, shopping malls, and theme parks were a distant future, yet we had things that kids today do not.

No air conditioning made backyard sleeping part necessity and, for me, all adventure. Dad kept an old bedspring and a mattress in the garage, and hauled them out on sweltering summer nights.

In those days small towns had single lights that flickered at street corners, too weak to penetrate backyard shadows. No ambient city glow leached out the stars. Nighttime was a delicious ebony that to a small boy, promised majestic revelations of wonder and mystery.

In the theater of the night I watched the best show in town with a cast of billions. Pristine stars danced and shimmered, only slightly out of reach. Mother bought a star chart with constellations. We made our beds, and looked for celestial shapes and designs. What a thrill to match drawings with formations in the sky. Soon, I could locate several . . . the Big Dipper was the easiest. I learned the story of Orion, the hunter, and his two dogs, Canis Major and Minor, following him across the southern sky in pursuit of Scorpio the scorpion, the summer constellation. Legend said that Orion died from the sting of Scorpio and now pursues him to settle the score. Above the North Pole I located Cassiopeia's Chair and Draco the Great Dragon coiling around Ursa Major, The Bear. High in the center sky was Taurus the Bull and Cancer the Crab. These and others became my companions as Mother retold the ancient myths that imbued in me the amazing awareness of an ordered universe.

The Perseids meteor showers came in August, just for my entertainment. The constellations marched in orderly fashion across the sky from season to season, but the meteor showers were syncopated streaks of fiery unpredictably. Oh, it was magnificent.

It was not that way with my own children. Cities were well lit and most of the constellations faded in the spectral glow. The world was more dangerous and sleeping outdoors thought less safe. Air conditioning and television beguiled us inside. Sadly, my kids never knew the magic moment when the dew rose from the ground so that even on the hottest night it became chilly enough to send you indoors. They never heard the distant hoot of an owl, cicadas sawing come-hither to their mates, or fell asleep to the love song of tree frogs. They missed the ineffable quiet that comes just at dawn, the eastern sky turns pink and, for a moment, the night birds hush, before morning warblers pick up the song to announce daybreak.

Several years ago, flying all night from western to eastern Africa, I awoke in the early morning and peered out the small window. There, only visible in the southern hemisphere, was the Southern Cross, just as I had seen it in my star book. I wept with joy in the slumbering quiet of a droning plane. God's wonder and majesty from the days of my childhood surrounded me in the gift of the stars. I was transported to that creaky backyard bed, and the clear, warm air of an Oklahoma summer.

The constellation slipped beyond my vision. Quietly I celebrated the memory of a mother's sense of awe and mystery in life, and who shared the awareness of God's grace surrounding my existence. I returned to sleep with a deep awareness of peace and wholeness. The universe, its wonder, its design, for all its astounding vastness, was a place where my friends, the constellations, played. I need never be afraid.

Recently a rare full eclipse of the moon was visible near our home. I eagerly awaited its appearing. That night was cold, the air chilly, the moon a burnished silver disk.

An eclipse takes time. It began around 9:30 and by 10:30 a darkening crept along the lower left edge of our satellite. Its brilliance began to fade. An hour later, as the earth's shadow inched over its surface, the night fell dark and hushed.

Gradually the eclipse advanced, leaving only a thin bright edge. It poised there for the longest time. I watched through binoculars. The moment the eclipse was total, stars hidden behind the reflected moonlight, popped into view. The orb hung in a three-dimensional heaven, suspended between earth and the far reaches of the universe. Like a smoky pearl, it dangled there in the sky.

Look up some clear, tingling winter night at the wheeling array or let the soft Milky Way blanket you for a hot summer sleep. Drink in the spectacle of creation. It's the best show in town.

MUCH OBLIGED

Clovis Eldon "C. E." Severe
Born January 9, 1896
Died April 7, 1971

GRANDPA JOHN SEVERE, DRAWN TO THE promise of land, signed up to join a wagon train to a new future. Oklahoma Territory was slated for statehood, and he and Grandmother Martha decided to be pioneers. The 400-mile trek from Harrison County Missouri would take almost a month.

The Prairie Schooner held all their worldly possessions. Most family members walked alongside, or rode a horse, rather than endure the constant jolting of the wagon on the narrow, rutted trail. On a good day they might make fifteen to twenty miles, but good days were hard to come by. Wagons were subject to breakdowns, and sickness might strike the whole assembly, delaying them for days.

When to leave Missouri was critical. The wagons must ford rivers – the Neosho, the Missouri and the Grand. It was impossible to leave when the spring rains overflowed their banks.

Bear Creek in Noble County, near their new property, was known to flood a mile wide. Still, it was critical to arrive in Oklahoma with enough time to grow food for the winter.

By June the rains passed. The wagon master said it was time. With four children between two and thirteen years old, they took their place in the column headed to Oklahoma Territory.

Land and the promise of a new state-a-borning awaited them.

At some point they moved from the farm to Hayward in Garfield County where they contracted to operate the community phone system. Martha became the central operator – until the main phone-board was stolen for the gold in the contact points. Grandpa John went to work in the oilfield. In the summertime they ran the concession stand at Hayward lake.

Oma, Lester, Clovis and Glen welcomed their brother Forrest, born soon after they arrived. Tragically, in 1905 sixteen-year-old Oma died of diphtheria. Otto was born in 1906. A family mystery concerns another child who died in infancy, supposedly buried in the family plot in Perry with no marker indicating its name or gender.

Before I came along, Uncles Lester and Glen moved to California. Growing up, I saw them only once. Otto's children, my cousins, were Don, Norma Jean, Leroy and John. Forrest married but had no offspring.

Norma, Leroy and I were in the Perry Marching band. Leroy played drums and my beautiful cousin

Norma was voted Band Queen and marched beside me the first year I was drum major. John served as drum major, later.

Of all John and Martha's boys, Dad was the runt. During World War I, while serving in France, the soldiers in his unit called him *Mr. Shorty*. He had bright blue eyes, and a warm smile. His face was less elongated than his brother Forrest, but not as round as Uncle Otto's.

As a young man he became a mechanic in a garage in Hayward. Mom lived in Perry and after they married he moved there, taking a job at Alvin Cockrum's Conoco filling station. At that corner station Dad was once robbed at gunpoint but, fortunately, was unharmed.

I was six when Dad purchased a Sinclair station. Through the Ethyl pump's glass cylinder, I watched the rosy liquid bubble down into gas tanks. It thrilled me to operate the long handle that siphoned it from deep underground.

Dad's station was a half-block south of our town square on Seventh Street. Down the alley to the east was a large Quonset hut that housed Charles Machine Shop. I found Charles Malzan's place intriguing. In the doorway of his building I played with the left-behind slugs – round discs knocked out of electrical boxes, pretending they were money.

Mr. Malzan invented several safety devices for oil well towers, including the Geronimo, an apparatus to pluck workers off of blown or burning wells. He ultimately became famous for the invention of the Ditch Witch that digs narrow trenches to lay pipelines and underground wiring. Later, during my traveling days, I was thrilled to spot Ditch Witch machines around the country and even on international trips.

Dad then bought the Sinclair Bulk Agency and became a distributer of gas and oil products to farmers across Noble county. The plant sat next to the Santa Fe railroad. I learned to ride my bike on the gravel street bordering the tracks, racing trains and always losing. This was during World War II, and the only toys I had Dad hand-made and painted with one of the company's logo colors, red, green or white.

In time the rigorous work of wrestling fifty-five-gallon barrels of oil, and the long hours of meeting customers' demands, took its toll on Dad's health. He had suffered from ulcers for some time and, in that day, there were few medications. But there was a doctor in Halstead, Kansas, reputed to be helping ulcer patients. I recall the long trips north and the boring day waiting while Dad was treated. Eventually medical science and surgery cured the ulcers. He was delighted to again be able to eat a bowl of chili. He also underwent several surgeries to slow the advancement of glaucoma.

After the war, Mom and Dad sold the agency and opened a neighborhood grocery store across from the Perry high school. My maternal grandmother had turned her small house, next to their store, into an eatery. She served hamburgers, chili, and pie. When her health faded she closed the café, and my folks took over the feeding of students. I was a teenager and able to help in the store. But I was a voracious reader and wasn't pleased when Dad interrupted me when I was deep in reading Dostoevsky's *The Brothers Karamazov,* or Homer's *The Iliad* or the *Odyssey,* because he needed a case of canned goods or a box of apples from the storehouse.

He loved to fish and hunt. Mom said that in the early years of marriage he might announce that he and Leon or Carl, or whichever buddy it happened to be, were going on a several-days fishing trip. On these occasions, Mom was not happy.

Dad was a good cook and was known in our town as a provider of food for large gatherings: sportsmen's clubs, Lodge meetings, Chamber of Commerce dinners and the like. His barbeque was excellent, as was his chili. He built a barbeque pit in our backyard and covered the outside with Barite Rose rocks. I especially loved his barbequed chicken, and still use his recipe.

In his late '50s and early '60s Dad began to have a series of light strokes. Eventually they became serious enough that he had to give up working. He was a near-total invalid for his last twenty-some years. But, when a stroke hit, he would exercise to recover the use of an arm or a leg. In 1971, at age 75, he died in the night between Maundy Thursday and Good Friday.

What was Dad like? He met people well, and his most constant comment when closing a business deal was, "Much obliged."

He was a laid back, easy-going person, with a droll sense of humor. When I was a junior in high school, it came time to order my senior ring. Dad said he thought it was too expensive and wasn't sure they could afford it. Secretly, he and Mom ordered the class of '52 ring and one evening at the dinner table he slipped it on his finger and, as he talked, kept waving his hand around until, at last, I saw it.

For having this kind and gentle man as my Dad, I am much obliged.

SHE WHO MUST BE OBEYED

Iva Rachel Davis Severe
Born September 3, 1901
Died March 29, 1992

MOM WAS SLENDER AND THIN-FACED AND, like her mother, bore high cheekbones, a sign of her never-spoken-of Indian heritage. Well into her senior years her hair was black before becoming streaked with gray. I never knew her to weigh much over one-hundred-twenty pounds. As grandmother aged, and then Mom, their skin took on the lovely patina of Native American complexions.

Mom was born near Blue Jacket, in north east Oklahoma. Her mother was part Cherokee, and her father Sac and Fox, although neither were on the Dawes roll. Later, they moved to Stillwater, where he was a finish carpenter.

I have often mused that, had I been told of her father's death by his own hand when she was fourteen, I might have understood her ever-present anxiety

She Who Must be Obeyed

over my brother and me. Following that tragedy, she, her sister Eva, and mother Nettie experienced hardship. They soon pulled up roots in Stillwater, where it had happened, and moved to Perry to start a new life.

My brother, Clovis Jr., was the firstborn. I arrived ten years later, an afterthought. Son, as Mom called him, was a quiet child. I wasn't. She told me, "I could place your brother on a chair and he'd stay there until I came for him. If I put you on a chair, you'd be under it before I got out of sight."

My hyperactivity, contrasted to my brother's docility, was not to my benefit. Mom, in her forties when I became a teenager, found her high-spirited child a cause for worry. My antics increased her resolve to control my exuberance.

I remember best the night of the long sentence.

Born in late October but enrolled in school in September before I became six, most of my fellow classmates were older. At thirteen, I was excited about what I believed to be my near adult status. I attended a party at a friend's home. Around ten in the evening someone said: "Hey, let's go to the midnight movie." I had never done that, but figured they all had.

I didn't call my parents for permission on this heretofore unheard-of late-night outing. More truthfully, I feared if I asked, the answer would be no, and I dared not risk having to tell the others I couldn't go. Attending the midnight movie sounded so grown up.

When I left the theater, at one-thirty in the morning, Dad was parked outside waiting for me. He tried to communicate the uncertainty of my near future, but it was difficult for him. He was easygoing while Mom was more uptight. Dutifully he delivered me home to her waiting wrath.

Her lecture was long, with my infractions repeated. I had caused her great pain and suffering the likes of which, in a court of law, could render a significant monetary judgment in her favor. In my disappearance she had imagined all kinds of calamity that might have befallen me. I'd been unaware that there was a circus in town plotting to abduct me to be their elephant boy. She insisted I was intent on bringing her to an early grave, and pronounced the sentence for my misdeeds. "From now on, young man, you will be home by ten p.m. – every night."

I deserved punishment. I assumed she meant until I was a little older, or had proven my ability to make sounder decisions. As it turned out, her curfew was intended for now and always. Her rule remained through high school.

It was clear she had called the party parents and knew all along I had gone to the movie, since Dad knew where to pick me up. But in her anger about my not calling, she acted as though I had vanished.

After that I never came in *before* ten p.m. My best friend, Ronald, often went home by nine. Not me. If ten was the rule, then ten it would be, even if it meant I sat on the stone wall across the street until the stroke of that hour. I learned creative excuse-making to cover any tardiness. I had lots of flat tires, which I'm sure Dad knew hadn't happened, but Mom didn't – he never ratted on me.

I well might have flunked out the first semester of college, for there Mom's rule was unenforceable. I could, and did, stay out as long as I wished.

Later, with our own children I used a different method. Once, when our daughter and her boyfriend stayed out too late, I met them at the front door wearing only my shorts. Embarrassment is a better corrective than anger any day.

Sadly, I was grown with children of my own before a cousin informed me of the suicide event that had so impacted my mother's world. By then, she was gone, and the opportunity to talk about it unavailable forevermore.

And even more lamentable was my not understanding her mood swings, her anxieties, and misplaced possessiveness, in between which times, she was a loving and caring Mom. I'm truly sorry I never knew.

GRANDMOTHER MOSSMAN

I GREW UP WITH ONLY ONE ADULT DEDICATED full time to spoiling me – my maternal grandmother, Nettie Gold Davis Mossman. In her eyes I could do no wrong and if perchance I had, it was obviously someone else's fault.

Born Nettie Gold near Bluejacket in northeastern Oklahoma, she was part Cherokee but never spoke of her ancestry. She married Kinzey Zachary Davis, and they had two girls, Eva and Iva. Once my mother alluded to the aversion that many Indians had to being listed on the Dawes Rolls, and I was left to assume that included her family. I deeply regret I never pressed Mom or Grandmother for more details.

Until I was grown it never occurred to me that Grandmother's features reflected her heritage. Most Native Americans around Perry were of the Ponca Tribe, slender and with darker complexions and a more slender appearance. Grandmother had characteristic high cheekbones. She was of medium height, with a round face and a serene nature. Yet there was strength about her reflected in her gardening, running her small café across from the high school, and her love of nature.

With Grandmother I found safe haven from the storms of life. At the age of eight, while jumping off a flat-roofed garage, I left most of my right ring finger, and a sharp-edged silver band, on a nail at the top. I told the neighbor lady who rushed to my aid, "Don't tell Mom, take me to Grandma!"

Across the street from the high school, Grandmother had converted her living room and kitchen into a café. Rising early, she made half a dozen pies from scratch, started a pot of chili or vegetable soup, and prepared for hungry students each noon. As a child, I was unaware of any food better than her cheeseburgers, French fries, chili, and a slice of coconut cream pie. I remain convinced of its superior position among the world's gourmet menus.

With help scarce during World War II, Mother became the office manager for Dad's Sinclair Gas and Oil Agency. Our home was on the same block as Grandma's and before I was school age, Mother took me there around 8:30 a.m. to spend the day.

I would help Grandmother prepare the hamburgers. She rolled five pounds of ground beef into quarter pound balls, stacked them in a large earthen crock, and placed it in her Philco gas refrigerator. When customers arrived, she placed the bowl next to the grill. As orders came in, she tossed one of the hamburger balls on the grill, placed a wide spatula on top, and smacked it with an empty RC Cola bottle that flattened it into a perfect patty. Flip, add a slice of cheese, swoop up toasting buns from the back of the grill, add a dollop of caramelized onions, and one had the juiciest cheeseburger ever tasted. Candy came in bulk – unwrapped and displayed in large jars. Though carefully rationed, I lived as close to heaven as a small boy might hope. Cholesterol had not yet been invented.

Grandmother had house rules. No smoking, and if she caught a student tipping his straight-backed chair against the wall, he might be banned for a week. No swearing either. She thought nothing of correcting a two hundred fifty-pound fullback. Sassing Grandmother earned permanent banishment.

She was tough, but tender. Her favorites were the boys on the wrestling team. She knew who was pulling weight and who could add a few pounds. She refused to serve pie to a wrestler who must not gain an ounce before the weigh-in. She attended all their matches and slipped along behind the bench, handing out Hershey bars for quick energy.

After lunch, each day, I napped while Grandma turned on the radio and listened to *Stella Dallas* and *One Man's Family*.

I knew Grandmother as Mrs. Nettie Mossman, and only after I was grown did I learn about her first husband, my mother's father, Kinzey Zachary Davis. He was a finish carpenter and worked on Old Central, the first building on the Oklahoma A&M College campus. My cousin John Whipple says he was Sac and Fox Indian. Upon his death, he was buried in an unmarked grave in Stillwater. Grandmother soon moved her family to Perry and started over. Eventually she married Henry Mossman, a local barber.

Grandma's traits can be traced to a deep-rooted appreciation of mother earth. In early spring she drove off in her vintage Ford Coupe and returned with a batch of wild mustard greens, lamb's-quarter and dock. She cooked these, adding a hearty cutting of turnip tops, a little sugar and bacon grease, and insisted that the family eat up. It was our spring tonic. During this season Dad, who rarely had a cold, avoided her kitchen.

Every fall Sand plums ripened along county roads, and by the time I was eight she took me to pick them and we made jelly. She dusted my legs, arms and neck with powdered sulfur to ward off the chiggers but we had to dodge the wasps. And, oh, the jelly was sweet and wonderful.

Grandmother never used a recipe. Be it a pinch, a tablespoon or a cup, she masterfully combined ingredients and produced cakes, pies, and other delectables. However, she did not pass her secrets on to her two daughters, and rarely allowed them in her kitchen. In the first years of marriage Dad did the cooking. In time, Mom became, as I always knew her, an excellent cook. She and Dad occasionally laughed over the remembrance of something mother had tried to prepare early on in their life together.

If one needs a model for being a grandparent, Grandmother Mossman would be a fine choice. She taught me to fish, to care for and love gardening–especially roses – and was my constant defender when Mother made me toe the line. Long after Grandmother's death, Mom told of great tensions that occasionally arose between them, usually over how I was to be disciplined. To their credit I was unaware of these conflicts.

Grandmother lived into her eighty-fourth year, dying quietly one day at my parents' house. I was grown, with a family of my own. I recall how matter-of-factly I received the news, gathered the family, and made the drive home.

In my theologically trained mind I reasoned that there was no need to grieve deeply. Grandmother was old, and had faced the possibility of a painful lingering death. She died suddenly – no pain, and no long stay in a hospital. Grief was present, but subdued.

A year later my father died. That was harder, but he had been sick for a long time. I thought I was doing okay dealing with grief.

We moved that spring to a larger church in Tulsa. I was a busy pastor. The children were growing. Paula was teaching in the Union School District. Life was good.

Some three years after Grandmother's death, I was making hospital rounds one day, walking down a long dark corridor at Hillcrest Hospital. I passed a room and casually glanced at the patient. I took another two steps and an image exploded in my brain. The woman in that bed looked just like my Grandmother Mossman. The force of this threw me bodily against the wall. My knees buckled, and I sagged toward the floor. I couldn't catch my breath. Tears flooded my eyes.

Slowly I regained my composure, ceased weeping, and walked back to peer into that room. The elderly lady in that bed looked nothing like my grandmother. I stumbled out of the hospital and sat a long time in my car, in awe of what had happened.

Unfinished grief had worked its way through the dark labyrinth of my memory. Unshed tears had waited – just out of sight.

That shattering experience was a blessing from my grandmother. It taught me to help others handle their grief and, if willing, to do so in a timely fashion. A few years ago there was a popular commercial phrase that said: "Pay me now or pay me later!" Grief is like that.

The Christmas after her death, we received Grandmother's last present – three quilts, one for each grandchild and one for Paula and me. She had handmade them and put them away with our names attached in a note, a cherished blessing and memory.

Grandmother Mossman was a larger than life presence.

Shouldn't all grandparents be?

A DAY WITH GRANDMOTHER MARTHA

MY FINGERS BARELY CIRCLED THE HANDLE of the churn. Dad's Mom, Grandmother Martha, and I took turns plunging and drawing the paddle in the round wooden box until the cream inside solidified into butter. When it was done, she poured the buttermilk into a jar, then used a spatula to mash the remaining fluid from the soft pile of creamy goodness, and shaped it into a mound in the butter dish. I was six, and spending the day at her house.

She had put her fresh-risen bread in the oven, timed to be done with the butter. Out of the refrigerator she brought home-made jam, and we sliced the crusty warm bread, slathered it with freshly churned butter, and topped it with strawberry jam. Oh, my!

Grandmother had been widowed nearly ten years earlier. Grandpa John Severe had died three years before I was born. They produced five children, four boys and a girl, Oma, who died at sixteen. When their father died, the boys insisted their mother move into town. She lived a few blocks from our house, and less than two from her beloved Disciples Christian Church.

One bitter, sleet-covered Sunday morning, Dad rang up to check on his mom. He got no answer. He waited awhile and tried again. No response. Another pause and a third ring and still nothing. With dread, as to what he might find, he started pulling on heavy winter garb – prepared to reach her house, under icy conditions. Just before leaving, he tried one more time and she picked up the phone.

Dad said, "Mom, where have you been? I've tried to call you for almost an hour!"

Grandmother replied, "Son, it's Sunday, I've been to church, where else would I be?"

No wonder it was said that First Christian couldn't open the front doors without Martha.

After lunch Grandmother's quilting friends arrived to work on their latest creation in the frame she kept in her front bedroom. I was invited to join them and sat on a high stool at one corner of the batting, and given my own needle and thread. I'm sure my stitches were taken out later, but I felt doted on and included by her friends.

Dad bought one of the first home Philco radios that made vinyl records. He captured Grandmother Martha singing, *In the Garden*. In time the 45 rpm was lost, but in my mind, I still hear her quiet soprano, "I come to the garden alone, while the dew is still on the roses."

Two years later, when I was eight, Grandmother Martha died at seventy seven. For reasons I never understood, my mother thought me too young to attend the funeral. I was disappointed, and curious about death, but more – I wanted to say goodbye to this tender grandmother who, for this grandchild, left us far too early.

AUNT EVA

AUNT EVA WAS MY MOTHER'S ONLY SIBLING and, as far as I knew, the role model for all aunties.

She insisted that my mother, two years younger, bring me to her house when we left the hospital. There Auntie could do what she did best, provide loving care and bark orders. And Mother had to do what she did least well, rest and be bossed by her older sister.

From early childhood, Eva dominated Mom. Grandmother dressed the girls as twins, and allowed Mother to skip a grade so Eva could watch out for her. Conflicts, resulting from this arrangement, marked all their days. Fierce love bonded them, but mother's patience wore thin when Eva came to visit.

Auntie would descend upon us and, while Mom was at work, launch into a frenzy of activities, move the contents of drawers, rearrange furniture, and discard items from closets. Mom was longsuffering and, when Auntie left, put everything back.

But Mom's flower garden became less than Eden the day Aunt Eva dug up and threw away her favorite Iris bulbs. Auntie went to the nursery and bought more expensive flowers. Mom blew up and, for weeks, grieved the loss of her plants. Auntie didn't seem to notice. She didn't intend to offend; it never occurred to her that anyone wouldn't understand her logic.

Auntie needed to be the center of everything. What happened to her was either the *worst* or the *greatest*. What took place in someone else's life was of little importance.

When I told her our family was going on vacation and would visit the Grand Canyon, in typical put-down fashion she said, "Oh, that's just a place to throw old razor blades."

Yet she could be caring. When my appendix ruptured before I was three and the doctors worried the sulfa drug might not drive out the infection in my small body, Auntie stayed with Mom and by my side day and night.

When Aunt Eva and Uncle Jim, a Woolworth store manager, were coming to visit I became wildly excited, for I knew they would shower me with gifts. Going to see them was even better. Uncle Jim turned me loose in the attic storeroom to play with the toys. Items were not yet shrink-wrapped or boxed, but lay in open shelves. Heaven couldn't compare.

I was oblivious to the raw edge between Mother's attempts to keep me from being overly stimulated, and my Aunt and Uncle's desire to indulge. They were fun and I knew I was special to them, even if Auntie was sometimes a wet blanket. My uncle was funny and a big tease. When a little older, I asked Mom why she never let me spend a week with them. They had extended that invitation many times. She replied that it was hard enough to calm me down when they left after a few days. A week was too much.

They often came to see us after exotic travels, sharing spellbinding stories. Their lives seemed filled with glamour and intrigue.

Uncle Jim only drove Buicks – the bigger the better. It was a thrill to ride in his shiny chrome-trimmed new car, which he seemed always to have. Dad's Fords or Hudsons couldn't compare. Uncle Jim's parade of sleek autos created in me a life-long fondness for new vehicles.

In time Auntie decided I was too old for toys. She proclaimed that clothes were a more suitable gift. The suitcases opened and out came not toys but shirts and socks and sweaters. I tried to hide my disappointment. I was not aware I had morphed into a new age. But Aunt Eva had spoken.

Such moments in life always catch us by surprise. One day you are too young to cross the street, and the next too old to play with toys. You are not seasoned enough to pastor the tall-steeple church but the next thing you know, someone younger than you is appointed there.

There ought to be a warning of such life-changing transitions, one last toy, or a parade. A band marches up to your house and a ringmaster invites you to climb into a golden carriage pulled by prancing horses. They haul you around the town square under a big banner that says:

CLOTHES – FOR – TOYS
GIFT PASSAGE!
or
MISSED THE LAST BUS TO
BIG CHURCH!

Cheering youths will line the streets. Knowing oldsters will shake their heads and wave wistfully. *You're now one of them.*

I'd like to think there was some hidden gift in Auntie's willingness to make decisions on behalf of the whole world.

Aunt Eva would have made a good ringmaster.

MISS LIGGON'S GIFT

WHERE DO PREACHERS COME FROM? As with me, most tumble out of the nurturing life of a local congregation. While my experience of God's call to ministry was dramatic and at a specific time, my whole life was an overture to that moment.

Becoming a clergy in The United Methodist Church involves a process of discernment, coupled with intensive education and supervision for years, culminating in ordination. Along the way there may be student pastorates, a kind of on-the-job training, but the span of time through college, seminary and an on-trial period can take a decade.

People hold different thoughts about how one becomes a Christian. Some believe you should have a deep, emotional, cathartic, experience of *conversion* for it to be genuine. You must be able to state the time and place in which you knew you were *saved*. Many worship services are carefully crafted to play on one's emotions. They use fear to bring on that life-changing moment. *If you died tonight, where would you spend eternity? Are you ready to meet God?* One then confesses one's sins, real or imagined, and is immersed. This is called *believer's baptism*.

Others proclaim that becoming a Christian is more of a *nurturing* process. A person's whole life is surrounded by the awareness of God's love. No fear is engendered and the emphasis is on life-long growing in faith. Infant baptism is widely practiced which asserts the child is enwrapped in God's blessings from infancy onward.

It was this second path that describes my childhood. I was baptized as an infant, and never felt the need to fear. My early existence was surrounded by a God of grace, not wrath. My life journey has confirmed that understanding.

By the time I was a teenager I had a growing awareness of my call. I became a leader in our youth program and delighted in going to district gatherings.

Summer camps were fun and I began attending them at Camp Pawnee when I was fourteen. Mornings were spent in Bible study or learning groups, afternoons in recreation and crafts, and evenings in worship. The last evening, Thursday, concluded with a plea to consider full time Christian service. As the worship ended we held hands and formed a long line, wending our way to a large lighted cross on a small rise of ground. As we sang, we circled the cross forming concentric rings. Then we were left with our own thoughts and decisions. No pressure, no cajoling.

The year I was sixteen, as we circled, the cross seemed to glow especially bright. I sensed my call to preach. There was no audible voice, but an inner conviction of what God was inviting me to do.

I sought out my pastor and quietly told him of my experience. He wisely cautioned me not to make any public announcement just then. He said when I got home I should share it with my parents and if, in a couple of weeks I still felt the same, to come see him. He wanted to make sure I wasn't unduly influenced by the emotions of the evening. Two weeks later I went to his study, and the journey began, or perhaps I should say continued.

So, during that summer, between my junior and senior years of high school, I confirmed the direction my life had been moving for several years.

It had begun in a loving, caring home with parents who nurtured me. Mother took me to Sunday School, and there, in my second-grade class, I met my teacher, Miss Liggon. She was to change my life.

Our classroom was small with a U-shaped table with just-our-size chairs and the teacher seated in the middle. Miss Liggon always met us at the door, greeting us by name and inquired how our week had been. That made each of us feel special.

She was a single woman in the community. We would have called her a spinster in that day. But she loved us kids and told us so and said that Jesus loved us. I could not recite any specific lesson she taught. She would not have considered herself a theologian, just a person who cared that small children learn about Jesus. That was her gift to me. By the time I left her class I knew that God loved me unconditionally. I need not fear God.

That gift has never faded from my life.

THE PAPERBOY

LATE IN 1946 I WAS OLD ENOUGH TO BE HIRED for my dream job . . . delivering *The Perry Daily Journal*. Twelve was the minimum age to be assigned a Social Security number, which the newspaper required.

On my birthday the Post Office issued me a SSN, and I proudly marched to the *Journal* office, and presented it to the personnel director, Mr. Harry Delashment. He printed my name on a file folder and slid my application inside. I expected to be assigned a route that day, issued papers, and sent out to deliver them. Sadly, no routes were open. When one became available, Mr. Sylvester, the route manager, would contact me. It was a long three weeks before that call came and I entered the ranks of the employed. I was delighted to be a budding capitalist.

Each day after school I hurried to the paper office. In that pre-TV era people expected their *Journal* before suppertime. Each edition was to land near the subscriber's door. If tossed farther away often, a complaint might be registered. Too many reports of missing or poorly placed papers and I could lose my job.

My daily supply was placed in a wooden cubby-hole marked with my route, number nine. I stuffed them into a white canvas shoulder bag and walked two blocks to my first customer. That gave me time to fold a number of papers to pitch on porches. The first delivery was to a grocery store. That copy was taken inside and handed to the proprietor, Mr. C. T. Talliferro. According to Fred Beers in *The First Generation*, Mr. Talliferro had made the Cherokee Strip run and had been one of few blacks to secure property in Perry.

Next was the newsstand run by Cap Swift who, in an earlier life, was the human fly for the famous 101 Ranch Wild West Show. He climbed the underside of the tent without a net as people *ooed* and *awed*. When the 101 went bankrupt, Cap drifted to Perry and stayed.

Bobbitt's grocery, the movie house, and the John Deere dealer followed before I began with homes that took me north toward the edge of town. Then turning west, I zigzagged south, finishing a block from our house. Most days it took an hour.

Delivering newspapers is an excellent first job. It teaches responsibility, introduces business skills, and gives one insight into human nature.

I purchased the newspapers from the publisher and resold them to my customers. I collected every Friday, giving patrons a coupon dated for that week out of my route book. My bill at the office was due in full each Saturday. If someone didn't pay I had to subtract their amount from my profits. Charity meant less income.

Weeding the Garden of Eden

Most remitted promptly. However, a few avoided me on collection day. When I knocked they never opened the door. Sometimes I heard noises inside, but no one answered.

Some had only a twenty-dollar bill, a large sum back then. They might owe forty-five cents, and expected change. If I didn't have it, they'd put off paying until the following Friday. One lady was particularly bad at never having small bills. Sometimes she did that for weeks on end. One Friday, I decided to be ready for her. I stopped at the bank and secured twenty dollars in quarters and, when I started to count out her change, she suddenly remembered she had some dollar bills.

I thought another customer too poor to pay. Their house was a two-story dilapidated structure of unpainted clapboard. The yard was strewn with rusted machinery and piles of junk. Except in the coldest weather, their five kids went barefoot, and I never saw any of them wear a coat. The father always dressed in greasy coveralls and oily driller's boots. The mother never appeared, but sometimes I heard her yelling at the kids.

For a while they paid promptly, but then fell behind. Because I believed them to be poor, I was reluctant to stop delivery or push them to catch up. So, I was carrying them at my expense. One day I was going over my accounts.

"Who is that?" my Dad asked, pointing to the longest coupon sheet.

I described the family on Kaw Street. "I know they're poor, but I may have to cut them off."

The Paperboy

Dad began to chuckle.

"Why are you laughing?"

"You're being bilked," he said. "That old man has money he's never counted. You go demand he pay you, and see what happens."

I rapped on the door. There was no response. I banged louder. Then it opened, and the man peered at me through thick glasses. Holding up the sheet of unpaid coupons I blurted, "I have to be paid for the newspaper . . . now!" It seemed a long while before he moved.

What would I do if he refused? What if Dad was wrong and he really was poor?

Slowly he reached into the bib of his overalls and withdrew a thick wad of bills. He removed a large rubber band and asked, "How much?"

"Err, ah, its forty dollars and fifty cents, sir."

He counted out four tens and placed them in my hand then fished around in his pocket for a fifty cent piece. I handed him the coupons and backed away.

Dad had been right.

He smiled, "Last month I watched him looking at a new tractor at the John Deere dealer. He decided to buy it and peeled off eighteen one hundred-dollar bills from that roll, and it didn't make a dent."

I had learned a lesson about standing up for my rights. And the surprising thing was that this encouragement had come from a dad reluctant to collect on long-standing bills owed him.

The two years I delivered papers were two of the healthiest of my life. I walked or rode my bike in winter and summer, rain or shine, and don't recall ever being sick.

Things were different when my son became a paperboy. If the weather was too wet or cold, his mother or I got up and drove him around his morning route. The papers, by then, only had to land in the yard.

I don't recall if I recounted my own paper delivering days to my son. Well – I may have mentioned it a time or two.

TRAIN WHISTLES

THE SANTA FE AND FRISCO RAILWAYS CRISS-crossed through my hometown. Huffing and chugging, work trains shunted full cars to be off-loaded or tugged empties onto a side track to be hauled away. Engines toiled back and forth hitching and pulling cars into one long line. As couplings engaged, screeching brakes at each change of directions caused a domino clank – clank – clank – up and down the line.

Each day the Texas Chief and Super Chief, steaming to Chicago or Houston, high-balled it through town. These silver-sided giants stopped only if passengers were getting off or boarding. When one of these monsters streaked past, we kids stood as near the tracks as we dared. Our legs trembled as the ground quaked and we thrilled when engulfed in its steamy fumes. If we caught the conductor's eye and pumped our arms to imitate jerking the whistle rope, he might give us a toot and a wave. What power.

I'd lie still in bed on muggy summer nights and try to pick up the muffled murmur of a steam locomotive as it approached far to the north. On steep rises, the engine rumbled deep and low, as if in travail. Rolling across the countryside the mournful call slid to a high pitch as it came closer, then charged – screaming full-throated through town, to the clackity clack of steel wheels on iron rails, and disappeared to the south. Each whistle grew fainter until it merged quietly with the night breeze. In the stillness of my room I pondered the faraway places the train would go, and wondered if I would ever see the world beyond that last whisper.

My home was less than a mile from the Santa Fe tracks. Its closeness gave me childhood nightmares. In a recurring dream, a locomotive jumped the tracks and chased me up Fir Street toward my house. My legs grew heavy – I could barely move them as the train closed in. I always awoke with a start. Except for Dad's snoring, the house was quiet, but I imagined I heard the faint grumble of a departing train.

Dad's Sinclair bulk agency was along the Santa Fe line. Petroleum filled cars were nudged next to our tanks. Because these deliveries arrived in the middle of the night, I never got to see an engine line them up under the rigging where gas was transferred to our storage units. I was certain, if I could be there at the right time, the engineer would give me a ride.

My play yard was our dusty gravel drive and the dirt road along the tracks. I learned to ride my bike beside those rails. I tried to keep up with the engine, but always fell behind.

After my brother went into the service I watched troop trains passing through. I waved at the young men in khaki uniforms, convinced that I would one day see *Bub,* my brother. I never did, but the GIs waved back and probably thought of younger siblings back home who missed them.

German prisoner-of-war trains rolled past, like huge cages, filled with gaunt-faced lads. Far from their homeland, they looked small and frightened. Here was the enemy and I was supposed to hate them, but instead I felt sorry. I waved and then felt guilty and unpatriotic.

On a Christmas morning during the war, when my brother was away, Dad went to the train station and found a stranded young soldier. He brought him home to share Christmas dinner. For a few hours he was the substitute elder brother and the son so painfully missed.

One stormy evening, when I was eight, my family drove to Enid, forty-five miles away. Heavy rain had fallen for days and the fields were saturated. We came upon a man in a bright yellow slicker waving a lantern, signaling us to stop. Dad pulled over. He was a brakeman – a real trainman. A swollen stream had swept out the railroad trestle and telegraph poles. The train sat some quarter of a mile from the highway and he had walked to hail a ride to town and report the washout.

To my wide-eyed amazement he crawled in the back seat next to me. Water dripped onto the floor, and he reeked of wetness and manual labor. I didn't mind. These were the smells of adventure. His name was Sylvester, (The same man who later was my route manager at the *Perry Daily Journal*.) and I was spellbound as he told about life on the railroad. Most thrilling, he taught me some signalmen hand signs.

The steam locomotive is gone, and today's diesel horns are uninspiring. Still, when I hear a lusty train whistle in the distance, I recall the magic of the rails in the still nights of my childhood.

UNCLE MATT AND THE CALF-RIDE CAPER

Dad drove his new Hudson Terrapin with Mom in the front seat and Grandma Nettie and me in the back. We left the county road and drove down the dirt drive alongside a neat whitewashed fence to the clapboard farmhouse. Along the front the porch floor slanted toward the water trough, where the family hound was lapping a drink. An ancient sofa was on the porch, and on it, waving, sat my Great Uncle Matt Gold.

He and Aunt Ollie were in their late seventies. Uncle Matt was the youngest sibling of my great grandfather, and the last living male of that clan.

I was five.

Getting out of the car I was engulfed in farm odors. Newly plowed fields gave off a rich earthy smell, but the hen house and pig sty were less pleasant. The barnyard reeked of animal droppings and wet hay. I began to sneeze.

In the distance stood a large barn whose sides once bright red, were now weathered to a burnished brown. The pitched roof reflected the sun like a dull mirror.

Inside the farmhouse coal oil lamps provided the only light. It was a warm and cheerful place. A black wood-burning stove dominated the kitchen. Steam puffed from the ever-simmering kettle. On the sideboard, Aunt Ollie had laid out home baked bread, fresh churned butter and dusky applesauce, waiting for a kid with a sweet tooth.

I was absorbed in the ambience of the farmhouse, ignored by the adults.

Then this small rough-hewn great uncle, with a face full of happy wrinkles, turned to me. "Well son, you've come at just the right moment. I have three young calves in the barn and was fixin' to ask the neighbor lad to come over and break 'em to ride. Since you're here I guess you can do that for me, now, can't you?"

I didn't know calves were not *broken to ride*. Uncle Matt also figured rightly, I'd be intrigued by his offer.

"Now, Matt," chided Aunt Ollie, "there isn't time for that. Dinner's almost ready. You folks wash up and I'll get food on the table."

A basin sat on the sink board, with a tall pitcher of water next to a cake of homemade soap. Mom nudged me ahead of the others, poured water into the pan, lathered my hands, rinsed and dried them with a flower sack towel. Others followed to *wash up*. I'd never been in a house without running water. Growing up in an almost antiseptic home, the thought of everyone using the same water to wash their hands was icky.

Uncle Matt and the Calf-Ride Caper

I'd forgotten about Uncle Matt's calf-breaking challenge. He hadn't. As we sat down to the table of country-cooked food, he raised the issue, and my anxiety. His eyes sparkled and danced. "You eat a hearty meal, boy. You'll need a lot of energy to break them calves."

On the one hand, I was scared out of my wits at the idea of anything that sounded so dangerous. Yet, would this sincere relative ask me to do it, if it was risky? Maybe it wouldn't be so bad, after all. Perhaps I was expected to do this task as the youngest person present. I didn't want to appear a coward. The prospect loomed dark, yet strangely fascinating.

I ate with gusto.

From his end of the table Uncle Matt spoke. "David, I noticed you ate well. I think you're ready to break those calves. Shall we go to the barn?"

The moment of truth had arrived. Would I give in to my base fears and beg off? As I pondered my options, Aunt Ollie broke the silence. "Matt Gold," she snapped, "you are not about to put that boy to breaking calves just after he's eaten. Why, the ride would be too much on a full stomach. You leave him be and let him rest a bit. Besides, we haven't had dessert. Those calves can wait."

I was grateful for the reprieve.

The two pies and the chocolate cake on the sideboard had not escaped my notice. No self-respecting country cook would think of offering her guests fewer than three desserts. Not wanting to offend Aunt Ollie, I had a sliver of each.

After dinner, everyone visited around the table. My stomach wasn't receiving well the two wedges of pie and slice of cake on top of the hearty meal. Or perhaps my mind had returned to my impending calf ride. Either way, I was queasy. I needed fresh air. I wanted to lie down. I eased out of my chair, went out on the front porch, curled up on the old sofa and fell asleep.

My slumber was not peaceful. In my dream three huge calves towered over me. Each was snorting and pawing the ground as if saying, *"You better not try to ride me."* Uncle Matt was in the dream too, standing by a calf, beckoning to me. I panicked and began to run. The calves chased me across an open field. I didn't know what they would do if they caught me, but I didn't want to find out.

Scampering up a rise I came to the edge of a pond and was running too fast to stop. I fell into the deep cool water. I came up sputtering and flailing my arms. The calves were standing over me, laughing.

When my eyes cleared, the faces belonged to Uncle Matt and Dad. I hadn't plunged into a pond – in my fitful dream I had actually rolled off the sofa, down the slanted porch floor, and into the big water trough.

Mother didn't laugh. She stripped me of my wet clothes and Aunt Ollie fetched big towels to wrap me in.

Uncle Matt said he was sorry I couldn't break his calves, but he'd call the neighbor boy to come over. Maybe next year I could come back. I smiled weakly and tried not to show my relief. Snuggled close to Mother on the way home, I slept.

I felt warm and safe and – well –a little sorry I hadn't ridden a calf.

HI, MR. POWERS

Had the Attention Deficit Disorder Syndrome been identified when I was a lad, I might have been their poster child. I was blessed with an abundance of energy, evident in the haggard look of my mother who was near forty when I was born. I was wired with high voltage inquisitiveness.

This played out in social settings as well. I liked people, kids, adults – no difference. Silence was not golden and I felt the need to fill all conversation gaps. When I was old enough I was taken to the barbershop and dropped off for my hair cut. Once, when Mom came to pick me up, Charlie the barber hurried out to the car to tell her that, during a lull in conversation, I had blurted, "We don't take baths much at our house anymore."

My buddy Jack and I, during our cowboy phase, loved to catch old Mr. Balen as he passed our corner as he walked to town and back. We'd hold him up with our cap pistols and not let him pass until he rewarded us each with a bit of chewing tobacco. The tiny pinch he gave us burned our lips and tongue, but we thought it wickedly grand.

While forbidden to cross the street, I did stand at the curb and greet passersby. Old Mr. Knifer, a German refugee from the First World War, lived at the end of the street to the west. He stayed in his house unless he had to go to town for something. He drove an old Model T that was loud and occasionally backfired. He never rolled up the window on the driver's side, and when I waved at him, he scowled and spoke in German, but it sounded like he was swearing at me.

Mr. Powers was the daily challenge. He lived in the big white house on the corner across from us. He owned The Noble County abstract firm downtown. He walked to and from work each day, taking a shortcut across the school playground. Each evening at 5:10 he emerged from behind the band building, hat pulled down and papers under his arm, angling across the intersection toward the sanctuary of his house. I was waiting. Nobody had told me he was a taciturn character, given to few words, but it wouldn't have deterred me had I known.

I began, "Hello Mr. Powers – hello Mr. Powers."

He looked at the ground and made no reply.

"Hi, Mr. Powers."

He kept walking, head down.

"Hello, Mr. Powers!" By now I was as far out on the corner of the street as I was permitted and he had to pass within feet. I added choreography by waving.

"Hi, Mr. Powers!"

In a near inaudible voice he muttered, "Hello, David."

I had received all I was going to get and by now he had reached his door and was gone.

Oh, well. There was always tomorrow.

THE VIRTUOSO

LIKE MANY MOTHERS, MINE LONGED FOR A child with musical talent. Culture was not an abundant commodity in our little community. However, piano lessons, tap dancing and tumbling were available. I tried tap and tumbling, but was dismissed for terminal oafishness. So, I was sent off to Mrs. Crowder to begin my formation as a piano player. I doubt Mom expected a Rachmaninoff, but may have hoped for a Frankie Carle. In either case she was to be disappointed.

Mrs. Crowder, a statuesque lady, wore strong perfume and too much make-up. Her purple-dyed hair was meticulously coifed. She was reputed to be an excellent teacher, which meant you were fortunate if she accepted you as her student. I was a challenge since, due to the climbing accident, I had lost a portion of my right ring finger.

The spacious living room of the Crowder home was her studio. We began with the basics, posture, proper hand positions, and fingering scales – all of which were reinforced with the slap of a ruler, should one slouch or use an improper form. After months of learning fundamentals and playing scales I was ready for the *John Thompson Book I for Beginners*. At last, here was something with recognizable tunes. By the second year I had advanced into Thompson's *Book Four*, and memorized several sheet music numbers. My progress was steady, if not stellar.

Mrs. Crowder presented an annual recital for second year pupils and beyond. This assured parents that kids were learning, and gave mothers the opportunity to compare their prodigies with less talented offspring.

The dreaded event was the watershed between the musically gifted and those destined to hum quietly and, for the rest of their lives, dust the piano. Embarrassment and chagrin followed a student's lackluster performance and our mothers would be relegated to a lower notch on the community's social ladder.

At such public performances one is required to dress up, an unnatural state of boyhood. Fingernails must be clean, trimmed, and buffed. Shoes shined, preferably with matching socks. These are not things boys volunteer to do – however, their mothers beam with pride when they sit down at the piano.

Each pupil played two numbers from memory. The first, a simple composition, intended to allow their inner butterflies to light. The second, a more difficult piece, demonstrated our musical gifts, if there be any. Also, each number was performed in two rounds, thus keeping dads in their seats for the full two hours.

I no longer recall what I presented first, but cannot forget my second number. Rising from the slatted folding chair, I approached the piano, faced the audience and announced I would play *Liebestraum* by Franz Liszt. Taking my seat, hands poised over the keyboard, I began.

This Hungarian rhapsody has three parts. The first carries the familiar tune most identify with the title. The second movement ends with a coda, which directs you to play the first part again but with a different ending that moves to the final notes. Then one stands and bows while the audience applauds. They always clap, either in acknowledgement of your talent, or in relief you're through.

The beginning went well. With pace and order, notes flowed from my fingertips. The first section was accomplished, the second proceeded, and the coda appeared. I returned to the first movement and headed toward the conclusion. But the transition notes for the closing would not come to my mind. In a desperate attempt to cover I replayed the coda and, with undaunted confidence, launched into the first movement once more. I thought another time around would jar my memory. If I didn't think about it, it might come naturally and I would move into the final passage.

But again nothing.

Surely, my mind said, *a third try will succeed* and I returned to the beginning. By this time only the musically challenged were unaware. Again, the fateful ending was near but my mind would not release the information. So, I simply quit, stood, bowed to the audience and, red faced, took my seat.

A few congratulated Mother on the fine job I had done, noting with just a touch of sarcasm that it was "such a long piece to play." Others mercifully said nothing.

The next fall, when it was time to start piano lessons, Mother sent me to a new teacher, Ms. Rodolph. She never mentioned why. Perhaps Mrs. Crowder refused to take me – or it may have been because the new teacher didn't recommend recitals.

Come to think of it, neither do I.

THE THING ABOUT BULLIES

EVERY TUESDAY WHEN I WAS ELEVEN, TO GET to my piano teacher's home, I had to pass the long tall hedge. And every week Tommy jumped me from somewhere in those bushes, pushed me to the ground, rubbed my face in the dirt, scattered my music and dared me to fight him.

Red-headed and burley, he outweighed me by twenty-five pounds. Skinny and weak, I was unschooled in the brutish arts. Sometimes he straddled my stomach and refused to get off, gleefully enjoying my squirming attempts to throw him. On those days I arrived late for my piano lesson, rumpled and dirty. There seemed little I could do but accept my fate and take the drubbings.

I didn't mention my plight to Mom until one day, in the scuffle, my shirt was torn and she demanded to know what happened. Explaining, I received no sympathy but a lecture on facing down bullies. Aware that she knew the difference in our sizes, I was bewildered by her admonition. Confronting Tommy only guaranteed worse beatings.

Summer arrived with blissful relief from piano lessons and the long tall hedge. I could safely stay in my own neighborhood.

Alas, a kid named Leonard lived on my block and our paths crossed daily. He bullied smaller kids but, as we were near the same size, had left me alone. One day he turned on me and for no perceivable reason hit me in the mouth, daring me to do something about it. I did. I ran home, tears streaming down my cheeks.

However, from the window of our living room Mom had witnessed the whole thing. She met me on the front porch, stopped me in my tracks and ordered me to return and exact justice from Leonard.

"You can't come in this house until you hit him back," she commanded.

What madness. I should run the risk of a pounding? *No thanks.*

Mom didn't weigh more than a hundred-twenty pounds, but could be fierce and, truth be told, I was more afraid of her than Leonard. I re-crossed the street with purposeful strides. He saw me coming and began to run. I chased him around a big house three times, caught him, pushed him down and hit him in the face, hard. Blood spurted from his nose and he started crying, which startled me into letting him up. Without a word he ran home. Awesome! I returned triumphantly to Mom's reward of chocolate cake bestowed like a victory trophy.

Over the summer I had a growth spurt. My arms grew longer, I inched taller, and while not hefty, I bore a new stature. There began to form in my mind an itch to take on Tommy. A year of unfinished business begged to be resolved.

That fall I was sent to the new piano teacher and no longer made the trek past the dreaded hedge. Tommy and I did not see one another except on the playground and neither of us wanted to add Mr. States, the principal, to our conflict. We had witnessed him belt-whip two boys twice our size for fighting on the schoolyard. I taunted Tommy, daring him to fight. We exchanged glowering scowls and sassy words, but nothing else. The year passed, as did we, into Junior High.

The new school building was across the street from my parent's grocery. By now Tommy figured out I was keen for a confrontation. And, true to a bully's nature, if I was the one pushing for the fight, he wasn't sure he wanted a piece of me.

I began to look for a way to have it out with him. I bumped into him in lines. Passing his desk, I nudged his books onto the floor. There was mutual harassment, but always short of physical blows. The boys' *fighting code of conduct* required him to throw the first punch.

The inevitable moment came one afternoon, when I challenged him after school. I shoved him . . . he didn't respond. Words flew, but he refused to fight. I reminded him of the days when he used to pounce on me, and of my intention to square that account. He jumped on his bike and started to ride off, leaving me frustrated once more. I picked up a rock and threw it at him, from a quarter block away. It hit him square on the back, knocking him to the ground. He was okay, but the blow brought tears. I watched him limp off, pushing his bike. It was enough. Case closed.

Bullies, be they boys or bishops, must be faced down.

TRADITIONS

ONE OF THE GREAT SONGS OF MUSICAL THEater is *Tradition* from Jerry Bock and Sheldon Harnick's movie, *Fiddler on the Roof*. Tevyev leads the people of Anatevka in explaining the strange customs of his people. The villagers asked, *why do we wear these little round hats, and why the beads on the end of our belt*, and the answer was, *Tradition!*

Several years ago, our bishop's wife introduced us to a Spanish custom called *Cascarones*. Egg yolks and whites are blown out through small holes in each end of a dozen eggs. Then they're dyed for Easter. When dry they are filled with colorful confetti and become blessing eggs. A family member selects a *Cascarone*, chooses someone who bows as the first person pronounces a blessing over them and breaks the egg. Confetti cascades over their head and shoulders. Our grandkids loved it.

The next year, our daughter called Paula to ask if we were going to do Cascarones again. Paula said it hadn't occurred to her.

"Well," Sherri said, "I overheard your granddaughter Chrissy telling one of her friends, 'we always do it – it's a family tradition.'"

Some traditions we practice for years but others remain unconscious to be recognized through some special event. That was true for me and picking pecans.

A pecan tree may grow to be sixty feet tall. It takes eight to ten years of nurturing before it produces a crop, but it may bear tasty morsels for a hundred years. During the summer and fall a green husk covers the nut. After a hard frost that outer shell turns brown, splits open, and pops out the pecan. Inside is the sweetmeat. Grandmother Mossman believed pecans were a gift from God. She used them in pies, cakes, cookies, and brownies.

After a cold spell, the pecans began falling along Black Bear Creek. This stately old grove of native trees was Grandma's favorite place. The owner was clever. Why should he pick up all the pecans when he could get others to gather them *on the halves*, meaning he kept half of what we picked, and we paid him for the ones we took home.

Grandma fixed a picnic dinner of fried chicken, potato salad, and bread and butter sandwiches, and her delicious peanut butter cookies. We drove to the Black Bear Creek and, after checking in, grabbed our gunny sacks and began searching. This was a kid's wonderland – a warm fall day, tall trees, the creek to explore and squirrels to chase.

Pecans, however, didn't drop on bare ground. They hid among leaves that had fallen. The brown nuts, with black markings, were difficult to spot. A long stick helped stir the leaves to find the prize. Soon I tired of stooping, picking up, and dragging the sack. It was time to slip off and play on the creek bank.

Traditions

At the end of the day the owner weighed our haul and we settled up.

Back home, the hard shell has to be opened and the meat picked out. For this, one needed a cracker, a pick to extract the small pieces, and a container for the sweetmeats. It was not a task for the impatient young or even busy adults and usually fell to older members. So, the task was Grandma's. After she died, the job fell to my mom.

One evening I was sitting in front of the fireplace with a newspaper in my lap, cracked pecans in a sack and a coffee tin for the meats. The year before Mother, at 91, had died. In our family I was now the oldest. Like Grandma and then Mother, I accepted the tradition of picking pecans. It was my turn.

My labor was not arduous. I picked with care. It was our tradition. I was moved, feeling the close presence of Mother and Grandmother.

Fortunately, our neighbors, Bob and Donna Merry, have a paper-shell tree with limbs that hangs over our property line. They say, "What falls on your side, is yours," and graciously share the bounty.

It is fall again and the leaves have begun to turn. Pecan husks are about to open. The winnowing north wind is rising. Maybe I'll pack a picnic basket of fried chicken, potato salad and bread and butter sandwiches, and go find a creek bank with a stand of pecan trees. Hopefully there is a friendly farmer there who'll let me pay him for the privilege of picking up his pecans and giving him half.

Wow, what a bargain.

MUDDY WATER SWIMMING LESSONS

MY CHILDREN AND GRANDCHILDREN learned to swim in pristine pools – crystal clear, chlorine saturated, and germ free. However, those pools were devoid of mystery, intrigue, and awe.

On summer afternoons, where I grew up, we waited at the high school for Humpy's truck to take us to the CCC Lake for swimming lessons. Humpy's truck was an ancient side-walled open bed Ford into which twenty or more boys would clamber for the four miles to the muddy old lake. Sometimes the transport was so loaded it strained as it climbed the steep hill between town and the swimming hole. Scrambling onto that truck for a bumpy ride and joining in the singing was part of the wonder of my childhood. No law, today, would allow kids on this kind of vehicle.

The truck belonged to Harold "Hump" Daniels, the high school football coach and history teacher. To us he was just Hump. He never thought of going elsewhere to coach, although he produced a number of state championship football teams. Countless boys and girls learned to swim in that murky lake. Hump knew and encouraged each one. I never heard of a drowning under his watchful eye.

The CCC stood for the Civilian Conservation Corp, a part of the Works Projects Administration or WPA. President Franklin Roosevelt created the program in 1935 to employ people during the Great Depression. They built roads, bridges, armories, sports stadiums, and recreation venues like our lake. It was great for picnics, fishing and swimming. The older boys said that it also offered secluded spots for lovers, but I wouldn't know about that.

There was no dressing room, no shower, and no concession stand. We carried a towel, wore our dry swim suits, and came back in wet ones. The evidence of our having been at the lake was a residue of red muddy water on our skin, sunburn and a slight fishy smell.

At the lake, we were divided into three groups – accomplished swimmers were free to go anywhere, even out to the raft anchored a hundred yards from shore. Intermediates could go beyond the safety cable, and we beginners stayed in the shallows until Hump had tested and found us to be able swimmers. Having to stay behind the divider provided an incentive to learn quickly. We ducked our heads under water and practiced arm and leg coordination while holding our breath to stay buoyant. In time we added kicks and strokes until we could really swim.

The deeper the water, the less likely you could fake it by kicking against the lake bed. Hump knew that and when you asked him to approve you, he led you out where, standing on tiptoe, you could barely touch bottom. Then he backed off about twenty yards and motioned you to swim to him. If you made it, you passed.

Then there was the matter of fish. The lake was well stocked, primarily crappie and sun fish. When we stopped moving, the little fry thought the hairs on our legs were delicious worms and nipped at us. Another incentive!

I passed the test. There was a certain pride as I left classmates behind and ventured out with the big boys.

Learning to swim was a rite of passage. I am grateful for teachers like Hump Daniels who knew the joy of acquiring a skill that enriched our lives. I would not trade that for all the crystal pools in all the subdivisions and all the gingerbread houses of this antiseptic land.

Encountering the unknown unknown in a muddy lake was to sense the mystery of life.

MY LAST BICYCLE RACE

W E BOUGHT WAR BONDS DURING WORLD War II, to show support for our troops. President Roosevelt challenged us to make sacrifices. Sparseness became a way of life. Mandatory rationing was imposed in 1942 following a failed attempt with a volunteer system. The Office of Price Administration, OPA, at the Post Office was where families received their monthly issue of rationing stamps for scarce goods, gasoline, sugar, coffee, and tires.

Our nation's resources were going into the war effort to manufacture airplanes, bombs, tanks, and ships with which to fight our enemies. Domestic construction was minimal. New toys, games and sports equipment – anything made of metal – were nonexistent.

After my brother enlisted, Dad stored his pre-World War II bicycle in a shed until I was big enough to ride it. The colors were faded and the name *Schwinn Commodore* barely readable. Being a Sinclair Bulk Agent, Dad had red, white and green paint available. Sanded and freshly coated, the bike was mine.

The bike had large thick tires, a solid steel frame and, one drive gear. It was no speed machine. I rode it to school, delivered newspapers, and with my buddies, peddled around town. All of us had prewar wheels.

After the war, new merchandise appeared, including bicycles. These were European in style with lite aluminum frames, and multiple gears and drive sprockets. The tires were light and thin, built for speed. Gradually my buddies replaced their older bikes with equipment that had names like *Blue Racer, Silver Streak* and *Lightening Wheels*.

However, my folks thought my old bike sufficient. Compared to the new breed it was like driving a tank. Racing friends was futile. When a challenger shifted into a higher gear, I was left behind. I avoided racing.

One day my friend Billy dared me to do just that. His bike had only two speeds – not as fast as those with ten. I thought I might beat him. We agreed on racing down the sidewalk, a block-long test of speed.

He got the jump on me and pulled ahead but I was pumping with all my might and gaining on him. I planned to overtake him in the middle of the block, swish through the tall hedge that ran alongside the alley, pass him and win the race.

Intent on gaining the lead I hadn't noticed the two-by-four upright in the end of the foliage. To avoid the post, I slammed on my brakes as I jerked the handlebars sharply to the right. The bike went one way and I flew into the air and onto the gravel alley, leaving a path of elbow skin. I was a bloody mess and carried the scars for years.

Had I been riding one of those fancy new types, it probably would have been destroyed in such a wreck. My ancient two-wheeler was unhurt, indestructible.

I never raced it again.

But it would be nice to see the old beast.

A LESSON IN RELATIVITY

TWO FACTS ABOUT MY SCHOOL CAREER remain undisputed. Math was not my cup of tea, and athletics wasn't my game. Boys were expected to excel in *some* sport. Football was the most admired, and the mark of superior prowess. The least appreciated was track.

Abe Lemons, perhaps the best basketball coach Oklahoma City University ever had, once said, *there's nuthin' to coaching track . . .you just tell a kid to stay close to the inside rail and get back as quick as you can.*

Mother forbade me to play football so I chose a close second. I'd be a wrestler. Over the years the Perry Maroon wrestlers have won many state championships. Olympic medal winners came from Perry. I was not among them.

Not that I didn't try. One day on the mat made it clear that my future wasn't in half nelsons or hip locks. My opponent slipped behind me, pulled my feet out, and dropped me square on my chin. As the pain subsided, and the gym lights came back into focus, I resolved to seek fame elsewhere.

A Lesson in Relativity

I tried basketball – suiting up, practicing and sitting on the bench most of the season. In this world of peer approval, if you got that far you were considered okay. I played in one game. It is probable that we were so far ahead or behind that it didn't matter. I was sent in with only minutes on the clock. My one chance for acclaim came in chasing a loose ball. I saved it before it went out of bounds. However, seconds before I ran after it, the referee's whistle had blown the ball dead. I was mocked for my ineptness.

Columnist Dave Barry, recounted his youthful chagrin at being unable to climb that infernal rope to the gym ceiling. I would add other impossibilities – chinning myself, multiple push-ups and all the humiliating competitions that separated the jocks from the ninety-pound weaklings.

Gym was required in junior high. This provided a daily opportunity for the coach to embarrass those of us who were athletically challenged.

Coach Divine had us put on boxing gloves, pair off and go three rounds of three minutes each. He matched us with someone of similar height and arm length. A long line of duos stretched around the room, taking turns stepping onto the mat that was the ring. There were no instructions on how to box.

Years before, while visiting my cousin Leroy, we'd borrowed gloves from a neighbor and boxed. I thought I'd done well. Being taller, and with longer arms, I had an advantage.

My partner that day was a boy who had recently moved into town. He seemed like a nice kid and spoke quietly as we waited our turn.

He asked if I had boxed before. I told of my one experience and returned the question. He nodded as he banged his gloves together menacingly: "My dad's a professional boxer. He's taught me a few things."

A wave of anxiety swept over me.

I considered declaring I was a hemophiliac, or a member of a church with strong anti-violence sentiments. In terror and dread I inched toward the mat. Oh well, nine minutes didn't seem that long.

I was putty in the hands of this neophyte mauler. He rained blows as I tried in vain to protect myself. By the end of the first round I wasn't worried about competition, just survival.

In the second round I considered feigning a telling blow and dropping unconscious to the floor. I turned the third round into a track meet. He couldn't hit me if he couldn't catch me. I think the coach enjoyed my misery and forgot to ring the bell.

In college I took a science course. The professor quoted Einstein as saying *time was relative*. Recalling that boxing match, and the longest nine minutes of my life, I agreed.

THE HUNTING DOG

ONE OF MY FONDEST MEMORIES WAS HUNTING with my Dad. When I turned twelve he bought me a double-barreled .410-gauge shotgun. We tromped the fields together and stalked the elusive bob white.

Quail season began in October when the days became shorter and the fall air crisper. Frost turned the foliage into bright golds and reds. Quail hid in the dense growth in hopes the dogs couldn't pick up their scent.

From my earliest memory, Dad owned at least one birddog. These unique animals are bred to smell quail, point and hold them in a bunch, called a covey, until the hunter *flushed* the birds into the air. If a bird fell, the dog retrieved the prey. In an open field his birddogs were a marvel of grace and beauty.

Dad rousted me before daylight so we could be at his favorite hunting grounds by sun-up. On the way I slumped in the seat of the bumpy pickup and tried to catch a few more winks. Cap, our dog, sat between us and seemed to sense when we neared the hunting fields. The second the door opened he shot past me and dashed off, eager to find quail. Cap liked to range far ahead of the hunters in wide sweeping arcs, moving back toward us, until he froze on a cache of birds.

Cap was a pointer. Traditionally, strong-willed, not easy to command, he became a statue when he located a covey. His body stiffened, tail straight out, one paw slightly lifted, nose pointing toward the unseen quarry. Together, Cap and Dad inched forward until the nervous birds – as many as twelve to fifteen in a tight circle – exploded into the air.

We could get off one or two shots before they flew out of range. At the gun blast Cap bounded forward in search of fallen birds. Gently taking a dead quail in his mouth so as not to break the skin, he returned to Dad and laid the prize at his feet.

Sometimes the fields were too dry to give off the scent and we could walk into a covey without warning. The resulting rise of beating wings provided a rush.

Cap always desired to get on with the hunt. He and Dad were always in a battle of wills, and he had to discipline the big pointer to find birds within range. This involved the use of colorful language, and if necessary a dusting of bird shot if Cap refused to mind. He had to learn his life was fraught with punishment if he ignored Dad, ranged too far, or over-ran a covey.

Once, Dad took our new minister quail hunting and arrived home empty handed. Mom asked if the fields were too dry for the dog to smell the birds. Dad replied: "Naw, but with the preacher there, Cap couldn't understand a thing I said."

The Hunting Dog

For some years Dad suffered mild strokes and, just before they got worse, was given a new dog named Jim. Before he could hunt with him, the doctor suggested dad's tromping-the-fields days had come to an end. He was torn about what to do with the new dog.

I needed a hunting dog like a turnpike needs potholes, but I rationalized if I took Jim it might ease Dad's feelings. I could carry on the family tradition. I brought the dog home.

Throughout the summer a trainer worked with Jim. He used a quail wing on a cord, and my new dog did fine. Jim could point the wing, and hold until I walked up behind him. I looked forward to a fine hunting season.

Opening day, my trainer friend and I took Jim out in the field. He had all the right signs of eagerness. When he came upon the first covey he froze on point, taut, beautiful. I eased up behind him. He quivered as I urged him to inch forward. The birds flushed, guns fired, two birds dropped. I glanced around for Jim. He should be bounding forward to retrieve the fallen prey. I heard a yelping and watched as my dog, tail between his legs, disappeared over the nearest hill. My new hunting companion was gun shy. Now I understood why someone had given him away.

I whistled and called, but no dog appeared. Finally, I picked up the fallen birds and we trudged back to the car. As we approached, there underneath was Jim, shaking and whimpering – on his back, with all four legs in the air. I crawled under and dragged him out. He wouldn't stand up, and I had to bodily load him for the ride home.

Not long after, I gave up both dog and hunting. I preferred to remember the sights of excellent animals working smoothly in front of my Dad, and the graceful rise of the quail.

In those days of my youth, birds were plentiful, the October sky deep blue, fields damp and earthy and the air so crisp our breath hung in ice crystals.

What greater memory could one ask?

A SIGN OF PRESENCE

SOUSA'S *STARS AND STRIPES FOREVER* OR A lead role in a high school play were more to my liking, than being an athlete. I played trumpet in the concert band, led the marching band as drum major and acted in school plays. Yearly each class presented a drama, and there was an annual all-school play. I read for parts and was cast in many of them.

While appreciated, even lauded by some, these activities received less esteem than that accorded the jocks. At class reunions the feats of championship teams are recalled. Cauliflower-eared old wrestlers and football stars with bum knees continue to be adulated for past victories. The marching band winning superior ratings at state contest in 1952 has never been mentioned. Don't get me wrong, many of those athletes are friends and I admire them. I'm just saying . . . .

At the end of my junior year this higher opinion of athletes was made painfully clear to me. Traditionally four boys from our school were annually sent to the Boys' State event, a prestigious gathering of young men to study government. Historically these slots fell to the captains of the football, wrestling, and basketball teams plus the drum major of the band. I had looked forward to participating. However, that year there were co-captains of the football team, and according to the whims of school leader logic, the drum major was eliminated so both football players could attend. What, me bitter?

My folks were proud of the band's half-time performances at football games and of me as the drum major. They came to watch me march in parades, and attended concerts and school plays in which I had a part. I never doubted their support for my activities, nor felt they were disappointed that I was not a jock.

During sports events there were football dads and moms who screamed their joys and jeers at the top of their lungs. Basketball referees were angrily threatened for perceived bad calls, and all knew whose son had been wrongly charged with a foul. Worst were the parents who corrected their kids from the stands. Mine were quiet. If I didn't land a part in a play they would not have dreamed of complaining to the drama coach.

Mom and Grandma would always be at a production but I never knew whether Dad would make it. The cast had to be in costume and makeup well ahead of curtain time and long before Dad closed his store. He might not come if a late customer loitered. Sadly, I never told him how important it was to me, for him to be there.

When the curtain rose, the footlights made it impossible to see individuals in the audience. However, Dad made a unique noise when clearing his throat, unlike anyone I had ever heard. It had a *huh-a-huhten* utterance, with a husky projection. Although it was not an intentional signal on his part, I listened for it. At some point in the play I'd hear that distinct sound and I knew he was there.

It was a sound of encouragement and a sign of his presence.

A SPECTACULAR FOURTH

ONE COLD FOURTH OF JULY WE GATHERED with our son and his family on a beach close to the Citadel Military Base near the Golden Gate Bridge to watch fireworks launched from boats in the Bay. But the San Francisco fog rolled in and instead of pyrotechnics framed by the bridge they had to aim them under the fog just above the water. That was spectacular in an odd way.

For years, on July 4th, our family had watched the Boston Pops Concert and fireworks on TV. We vowed someday to see it in person. Finally, one Fourth we made it to Boston. Early that morning we walked to the Charles River and the bandshell where the Pops would perform. Returning to the park in late afternoon we discovered what all Bostonians knew – we should have stayed and staked a claim on somewhere to sit. The place was a mass of humanity. It also turned out to be a miserable 100-degree, breezeless evening, and not an inch of ground unoccupied. We trudged back to our hotel, listened to the concert on television and watched the fireworks from our balcony.

The day worth remembering, while not as thrilling as a lift-off at Cape Canaveral or the eruption of Mt. St. Helens, was extraordinary for my hometown in the mid-'50s.

The Fourth was celebrated with a parade around the town square. The American Legion color guard led, followed by the High School Marching Band and the Saddleback Club. If the Band was lucky we marched ahead of the horses. Otherwise, demonstrated fancy footwork to avoid the droppings.

Next, kids on bikes pulled pets or younger siblings in wagons, followed by patriotic floats. The mayor, and other city officials, road in cars. Veterans of World Wars I and II marched ahead of a few jeeps, a troop carrier, and a vintage cannon pulled by the Boy Scouts. Last in the parade was the city equipment trucks, and, with siren yelping, our big red fire truck.

We were proud of our veterans. World War II had ended a few years before, bringing an influx of younger G.I.s into the thinning ranks of World War I veterans. Some marched beside their fathers who had served in the first Great War. The neat crisp khakis of the most recent vets contrasted with the ill-fitting uniforms of older soldiers. We respected these people whom we believed had gone off to save the world for democracy.

After the parade everyone gathered at the band shell in the square to hear patriotic orations. Occasionally there were visiting dignitaries, but mostly the speeches were by home folks. Politicians were drawn to such events like flies to warm watermelon. They would *hold forth* on the great job they were doing and declare that their re-election, come November, was critically required.

In the evening, after the sandlot baseball game, there was a fireworks show culminating in a fiery display of the American Flag as the P.A. system blared *Stars and Stripes Forever.*

Fireworks were sold from stands around the town square, there being no city ordinances against it in those days. Nor were there rules forbidding setting them off inside the town limits. From early morning to late at night we heard firecrackers, dodged sidewinders and watched soaring pop bottle rockets.

There were fireworks tents in front of the two five and dime stores. Mr. Holland was the manager of the McClelland's store on the north side of the square. Mr. Limery managed Kress's on the east. A rivalry developed between them to see which one's booth sold the most. They agreed to an inventory after the day was over. No one ever knew if more than bragging rights were on the line, but in the days leading up to the Fourth, they spied on each other to see how sales were going. It was rumored that Mr. Holland was slipping a few dollars to some kids to buy at his tent.

The day worth remembering began like most Oklahoma July days – hot. The air was heavy, just a hint of a breeze. The sun bore down from a cloudless sky as the parade formed along Delaware street at the northwest corner of the square, lining up west toward the high school. Parades always began there, turned south on Seventh Street, marched another block to Cedar, east a block on the south side of the square, then north on Sixth back to Delaware. From there west to the beginning corner, turning north on Seventh to disband. Only four blocks, so it wasn't a great parade, but it was ours, and the town was full of citizens from all over the county and beyond.

The high school band made a left turn at the final corner and marched to the band shell in the center of the town square. They continued playing as the crowd gathered for the patriotic speeches and festivities.

The Star-Spangled Banner was played, one of the older veterans led the Pledge of Allegiance, and Rev. Lorenzo P. Hargess of the First Southern Baptist Church gave a protracted invocation. Several speeches followed. Finally, Colonel Cranston Kelly, a World War I veteran, began his annual recitation of the poem *The Battle of the Marne*. He was telling of the bombs falling around them in the French trenches, when it happened.

Over at Kress's someone lit a roman candle and accidentally turned it toward the fireworks stand. Two incandescent globs of colored fire landed on the display inside, instantly igniting other explosives, setting off volleys in all directions. The attendants jumped over the counter and ran to safety as the crowd, waiting to buy fireworks, scattered, and dodged a hail of bottle rockets.

Aerial rockets burst through the top of the tent. Red chasers writhed on the ground, screaming and spitting fire. Strings of firecrackers ignited and sounded like machine guns. Sky rockets arched into the park and exploded near the bandstand. The large cannon pieces detonated. More roman candles puffed their fiery loads into the sky.

At the bandstand, bedlam erupted. Mothers snatched up small children, some of whom were running toward the noisy fireworks. Colonel Cranston Kelly, being mostly deaf, did not hear the explosions and went on reciting. One older veteran, who had fallen asleep, woke with a shout, "The Jerrys are attacking," and flattened the mayor on the ground yelling, "Get down, you fool!"

Though the volunteer Fire Department swung into action, they had never fought anything like exploding fireworks. They were not sure if water would work but it was all they had so they advanced on the blaze – hoses at full force. In a short time, the fire was out, the stand a soggy limp mess.

There were no more speeches. The band marched off to the High School. Veterans went home to change clothes. And the kids were soon back, shooting firecrackers.

Mr. Holland insisted that he had won the war of the fireworks, but Mr. Limery claimed that he had prevailed since there were no leftovers to be counted.

These days you can't shoot firecrackers inside city limits, and few are around who remember the day the stand blew up.

But I was there, and I can tell you, it was a spectacular Fourth.

THE LOST DRUM MAJOR LESSONS

WORLD WAR II ENDED AND AMERICAN soldiers came home with dreams of recovery and prosperity. Life would return to normal. But a new enemy arose, this one not flying airplanes or driving tanks. Polio! The epidemic of the 1940s and '50s struck down thousands.

Medical science couldn't tell us where the disease came from or how it was contracted. There was no cure. Someone opined it lurked in lake water, and kids, forbidden a cool dip, sweltered through hot summers. Others said the malady was borne on the evening air, so at dusk citizens scurried inside and shuttered their homes. Out of fear, folks avoided crowds and community gatherings.

Some victims died quickly. Others lived, but depended on iron lungs for every breath. Those that survived had twisted and deformed legs, and hobbled in braces with canes. When it struck someone you knew, they were quarantined and you could never go see them.

To find a cure for infantile paralysis, President Franklin Roosevelt, himself a victim of the disease, created the National March of Dimes Campaign. By the early fifties, scientists were working on anti-viral solutions, but it would be mid-decade before Jonas Salk came up with a vaccine that eventually wiped out the disease, globally, for nearly a century.

Johnny Skinner was a polio survivor. Although the malady stunted his growth and left his legs nearly useless, he was determined to rise above his handicap and re-learn to walk. He became the spokesperson for Perry's annual March of Dimes Drive, pressing everyone to donate. At first people were wary of getting close to Johnny, but his outgoing personality and persuasive spirit won everyone over.

In my junior and senior years of high school, I was the drum major of the marching band. We performed halftimes at home football games. In a typical show we executed the letters PHS, for Perry High School, and played our school song. Mr. Lemler, our director, didn't care for fancy footwork, or jazzy halftimes. He preferred clean straight lines stepped to the cadence of a Sousa march. Nothing thrilled him more than when each rank hit the yard lines at precisely the same moment. He said: "A marching band should march, not sashay."

On one occasion he relented and agreed to our doing what was known as the "Lost Drum Major Act." At that halftime we moved crisply to the fifty-yard line, turned sharply toward the home stands, formed the school letters and played our school song, *"Dear Old Perry High."*

I then directed the band to face center field and execute a *column left*. They turned right. After a few yards of marching alone, I feigned surprise, blew my whistle shrilly and ran to the front and signaled them to halt. Instead they performed a to-the-rear march. Again, I rushed to get ahead of them – to no avail. Whatever I commanded the band did the opposite. The fans were laughing uproariously.

Finally, from the sidelines a small figure shuffled out on the field. It was Johnny, dressed in an oversized marching uniform, and carrying a plumber's helper for a baton. He swung in front of the band and motioned them to forward march. To the exuberant cheers of the crowd, they followed him off the field, with me trailing dejectedly behind.

Johnny taught our community not to fear the unknown. He persuaded us to give generously to a cause that was greater than ourselves. He demonstrated that spirit and sheer grit will move us above self-pity and life's circumstances.

THE BAREBACK RIDER OF NOBLE COUNTY

IT SOUNDED LIKE FUN WHEN MY FRIEND Raymond Beasley invited me to go horseback riding. I knew little about farm animals, especially horses – the same for cows, goats, sheep and other denizens of rural life. But the idea of riding a steed out in the countryside was awesome.

Ray was something of a wild fellow who loved doing daring things. He once took a bull whip to a nearby community noted for being unfriendly toward folks from our town, thinking this weapon would intimidate the toughies. He came home badly beaten and sporting two huge black eyes. He reveled in the experience and loved re-telling the fight. Knowing this, I should have suspected the day would include something more than a quiet excursion.

We rode our bikes to the farm. Waiting were two horses, two bridles and bits, but only one saddle. The other, we were told, was a mile away at another ranch.

"No problem," assured Ray. "You take the saddled one and I'll ride bareback."

So off we rode to retrieve the missing tack and begin our bucolic adventure. Raymond led the way. It did not occur to me to question why the two horses were together, minus one significant piece of equipment.

Halfway to the other farm Ray stopped to rest. He said riding bareback wasn't difficult, but did require a break now and then. After a spell he said: "Lets trade off. I'll let you ride my horse for a while." He made it sound like he was doing me a favor. It seemed like an innocent offer, notwithstanding I had never ridden a saddled horse before, let alone bareback.

Boosting me up, he jumped astride the other one and took off with a shout. He knew full well that my beast was by nature a leader, not a follower. When Ray spurred his ride, my horse's ears quivered, and then laid straight back, and he bolted after the fleeing steed. He was not about to be in second place.

Down the road we sped, with Ray whooping and urging his horse faster and faster. My horse, determined to overtake the other, was paying no attention to my feeble attempts to slow him. I rolled back and forth across his broad back. Frantically I clung to the reigns and the horse's mane for dear life, all the while screaming at the top of my lungs "Whoa!"

Finally, we stopped and Ray collapsed in a fit of laughter. I slid to the ground and hugged it like a lost friend. He was extremely pleased with himself for setting me up. I missed the humor in it and, had not strength failed me, would have parted his skull with a rock.

We traded back and arrived at the other farm to retrieve the second saddle. For some time, after that day, Ray would grin at me and ask if I wanted to go riding.

I never did.

MOM'S SADDEST SONG

AT AGE EIGHTEEN MY OLDER BROTHER BUB enlisted to fight in World War II. My loneliness was profound. My Mother, a natural-born worrier, constantly fretted that something would happen to him. Millions of other mothers felt the same.

Military mail was infrequent, but not a day passed when Mom did not expect a letter from her son. In the darkening evenings, we tuned the radio to H.V. Kaltenborn's and Walter Winchell's war reports. Those years were one long, gray, winter, punctuated by bright moments when a letter arrived, or the war news seemed favorable.

For Mom, the saddest occasions were Bub's birthday and Christmas. We didn't need the calendar – she was a walking announcement. She became restless, didn't sleep, and paced from one end of the house to the other in the night.

Mom played the piano, haltingly. Her favorite was *I'll be Home For Christmas* written in 1943 and recorded by Bing Crosby. It was a song of promise and hope – a guard against the gripping dread. Often, when I came from school she would be at the piano playing and crying. To this day I hear it and remember that small woman, in her disconsolation, singing her song as a plea to the gods of war to spare her son and return him safely,

> "I'll be home for Christmas,
> You can plan on me..."

In time Bub came home, and while not wounded physically, returned to fight a life-long battle with alcoholism. It wouldn't be fair to blame his addiction on the war, nor did he. But it began there, and it would be more than twenty years before he and Alcoholics Anonymous would wrestle that demon to the ground.

We forget how terribly long it took to get news from loved ones in that pre-electronic-digital age. Today the immediacy of television doesn't lessen the fear of parents whose child is in the service. But e-mails, skyping, and Face Book are common between battlefield and home. During Desert Storm I heard of a family whose phone rang in the middle of the night. It was their son, somewhere in the Middle East. His unit was deployed through the desert, clearing out small villages. In one he'd seen a public phone hanging on a post. He picked it up and dialed his home number. To his amazement, the call went through.

No such communications were possible during WW II. Letters, heavily censored, took weeks to arrive, and even longer to be delivered to soldiers. Christmas packages, some soldered inside large spam cans, were mailed in July or August in hopes they would be there by December 25th.

"I'll be home for Christmas
If only in my dreams."

Mother played against the darkness of days filled with anxiety. She forced the words out of her deepest being, to be shafts of light and pretend bravery.

Each Christmas I hear and receive that song gratefully, in memory of a tiny woman for whom it was a defiant cry, a prayer of supplication, and a hymn of hope.

THE PASSING OF THE NEIGHBORHOOD GROCERY

GONE ARE THE FILLING STATIONS WHERE your gas was personally pumped by an attendant who checked the car's oil level and washed the windshield. No more the corner drugstores where the clerk topped your ice cream cone with a red candy cherry and the haberdashery that altered your new suit for free. And gone are the mom and pop neighborhood groceries. These have vanished from the scene, taking with them an era of commerce infused with customer care and gentility.

When Mom and Dad ran the Sinclair Oil Agency and a farmer needed a product late at night or at the crack of dawn, Dad delivered it. There was no "I can get that to you next Tuesday between one and six." It's likely that the breaking of Dad's health, while he was relatively young, was the price he paid. But, no mind – service was his stock in trade. And his standard response to a customer was, "Much obliged."

When Dad could no longer wrestle the fifty-five gallon barrels of oil, they sold the agency and put in a neighborhood grocery store. Chain grocers first appeared in the metropolitan cities while smaller communities continued to supported family-owned stores. Locals walked a few blocks to purchase their food.

Our store was across the street from the high school and next door to my Grandmother's house, part of which she had converted into a small cafe where students could purchase a hot lunch. When she closed her cafe, my folks altered part of their store into a lunch counter – selling sandwiches, chili and soft-serve ice cream from the first such machine in Noble County.

For that era, our grocery store was full service – including a fresh meat counter. The problem was that, if the meat did not sell quickly and began to discolor in the case, it became our next meal. Our family joked that beef steak should be aged to black before it was proper to eat.

A box of bananas came to our store as one stalk with thirty or more bananas, mostly still green. As they ripened we picked them for sale. I used to pluck bright yellow ones for me and my next-door buddy Jack Sveland, and then I'd pick a tiny green one from the end of the stalk to give to his little brother, Billy. The alum in the unripe fruit made him pucker up, which Jack and I found great fun. Amazingly Billy wound up in the food business.

An avid reader, I devoured books, from Albert Payson Terhune's *Lad, a Dog* to the Russian Dostoevsky's long sagas and the Greek myths. This became a source of irritation to Dad. All I wanted to do was read, while he needed me to stock shelves. He sent me to the storeroom for a carton of canned corn, which I put on the shelf, then returned to my book. I'd be engrossed in an exciting chapter and Dad would send me to get something else. I'm sure there was great sighing and eye rolling on my part as I did, reluctantly, what I should have done without being asked.

My daily assignment was to clean the soft-serve ice cream machine. Unfortunately for my waistline, it was too tempting not to eat the leftovers. Since no one else in Perry had one of these new inventions, our store was popular. I remember my math teacher Mrs. McCubbins, a prim, gray-haired lady, standing at our lunch counter eating a Frito-chili pie – a scoop of chili spooned into an open bag of corn chips – then ordering an ice cream. She savored each bite of the cone, and daintily dabbed her lips with a napkin.

While my mother was not impressed with people of position or wealth, Dad was warm and friendly with everyone. Mrs. Gerard may not have been rich, but she had more than most, and didn't mind you knowing she felt entitled. She drove the latest Chrysler, and bought large quantities of canned foods. But I never knew her to set foot in the store. She'd call and order full cases of fruits and vegetables. When she drove up and honked, she expected Dad to carry everything to her car. Mom seethed over what she viewed as a privilege extended only because *Mrs. Gerard thought she was better than everyone else*. Dad said her money was as good as anyone's and she spent a lot of it at our store.

I credit our neighborhood store with softening my Dad's attitude toward Roman Catholics. He was an active Mason and had misgivings about the

Catholic Church. Perry's St. Rose of Lima was about two blocks from our store. It was understood that Catholics, especially the priest's housekeeper, were supposed to trade and charge groceries at Lindeman's about nine blocks away. But, on occasion the housekeeper, Ms. Kennedy, pressed for some item, dropped by our place for a quick cash purchase.

Gradually she discovered it to be a safe place where she could vent her frustrations. One day she sighed and said, "Well, Father said mass in his pajamas again." A friendship developed between her and my folks – until she retired and moved to a town in western Oklahoma. At that time, we lived in far southwest Oklahoma and the folks came to see us but left early so they could go by and visit with her.

In his early sixties, Dad began to have a series of strokes. When they became so bad that he could no longer work, Mom ran the store for another ten years. Eventually the school system wanted our land for new buildings. For a while Mom resisted, but she was getting tired, and when the school board hinted they might use the law of eminent domain, she folded and sold our house and the store.

Chain groceries began to appear. Friends of my folks, the Galloways, also had a small grocery in a different part of town. They too faced closing, dealing with their age and competition from the new Safeway.

An era was passing. Mom and pop stores were exiting the scene. They were where folks not only got their daily provisions, but where troubles were shared, care was extended, and friends just visited.

A sweet life while it lasted.

FIRST LESSONS IN POLITICS

WHEN THE SCARCITY OF GOODS EASED after World War II our high school acquired a new sixteen-millimeter film projector. Mr. Divine, the Principal, trained several of us boys to set up the machine, thread the film – then hook it into the take-up reel, focus and run films. We were the projectionists for assemblies and classrooms.

One day I was asked to take the equipment to the Country Club and show a movie for a men's dinner. My family could not afford a membership in that select clique and the only time I ever went there was in summer, to be a caddy. I had never been in any other part of the building except the pro-shop, certainly not the dining area.

As the men came in, I recognized leading citizens of our community – the mayor, a dentist, business owners, a banker, and a couple of City Council members. Several were pillars of my church, First Methodist.

I was shocked when some of these men appeared from a back room with glasses of liquid that did not look like Coca-Cola. This was before liquor-by-the-drink and prohibition was still in force in Oklahoma. There was no disorder, but I'd never been present in a public place where alcohol was freely consumed. It was my first lesson that some people in town enjoyed privileges not available to the average Joe.

A second lesson came when a group of us kids began to talk about Perry's need for a community swimming pool. We discussed how to get our City Council to provide what we saw as an obvious improvement. We hadn't a clue as to what it would cost, and knew even less about how it would be financed. But after several meetings, our enthusiasm grew, and we passed petitions hoping to get enough signatures so the city leaders would agree to our proposal. People all over town signed. But now what? Did we just take these forms to a Council meeting? What if they wouldn't listen to us?

The father of one of the kids in our group, Mr. J., was an attorney. He agreed to represent us at the next Council meeting. We began making plans to celebrate our victory.

The Council heard Mr. J.s presentation and said they would take it under advisement. We thought that meant we'd hear something in a day or two. No, they would put it on the docket for the following month's meeting. We were disappointed but hopeful.

The next meeting came and went – no action on our pool.

Then mid-way in the following month we learned that the Council had decided not to consider it now – or ever. We gathered in disbelief. How could they turn us down? We'd gotten enough signatures to convince them that there was wide support for a civic pool.

After the meeting I went home in a foul mood, which Mother picked up on and sat me down at the kitchen table. "David, do you want to know why this didn't work?"

I nodded.

"In all communities there are political differences. There are Republicans and Democrats, and some are in power and others aren't. I'm afraid your cause was lost because you had the wrong attorney. You see, Mr. J. is not well thought of by our current political leaders. Your pool was turned down, not because it didn't have merit, but because they were not about to allow Mr. J. to be a winner – on anything."

Over the years, in many small towns, I've seen this pattern multiple times. A good idea, by itself, was never sufficient – if the wrong crowd proposed it.

Then there was Mr. Hicks, a would-be politician, and a good friend of my folks. Time after time he filed for a variety of Perry's political positions – always going down to defeat. And in each attempt, he'd been unblinkingly convinced he was going to win. He would drop by our house and with great confidence hold forth on what he was going to do *after he was elected*. My folks listened and offered muted encouragement which he always interpreted to be their enthusiastic endorsement. The truth was he had no wide-based support group and after years of failure his annual *run* became a community joke.

Others, seeking office, could only hope they drew Mr. Hicks as their opponent.

The church, like all human organizations, is not above politics, although I have met many of the faithful who pretend it doesn't exist.

Politics in all human-run organizations is a reality, and striving for what one believes is God's will, has rarely received a unanimous vote.

MAKING AN
AUDIENCE DISAPPEAR

A MUSE AND BAFFLE YOUR FRIENDS, the magazine ad promised. *For only two dollars you can master mystifying card tricks and sleight of hand.*

When *Magic Made Easy* arrived some weeks later, I devoured it and began to practice what would become my life's passion. Magician Harry Blackstone would quake in his top hat if he knew. I was destined for stardom. I was twelve.

However, with a finger missing on my right hand it was not easy to perform the most elemental illusions of the trade – palming a card. However, I developed an act I could present convincingly. I hungered for more, and the letter I received said that if I ordered Volume Two, of *Magic Made Easy,* I would be amazed at my next level of prestidigitation. To attain that higher skill would cost me three dollars – a paltry sum for such heady promises.

More Magic Made Easy turned out to be disappointingly much like Volume One. There were new card moves and more difficult sleights of hand, but I longed for bigger things. Magicians on television used special equipment – rabbits pulled from top hats, silver rings that linked and unlinked at the will of the man in the shiny tuxedo. Silk scarves appeared from thin air, and disappeared as quickly. I had no clue.

Then fate took a hand. On a trip with my grandmother to visit my aunt in Louisiana, we had a layover in Oklahoma City at the Union Bus Station. While waiting for our bus I wandered to the end of the block to find, on the first floor of the Black Hotel, a Magic Shop.

Stepping inside I inhaled a faint aroma of incense and from somewhere a flute played a haunting tune. Electrifying paraphernalia filled the shop – silk top hats, a must for a successful act, capes, wands, canes, colored scarves and magical devices too wonderful for me to guess their use. A tall thin-faced man stepped from behind a black curtain. He stretched a long bony arm and tweaked my nose, and out fell coins.

A sign on the wall said, *The Amazing Mr. Gene*. He performed trick after trick, assuring me that whatever I bought he would teach me how to present, and would tell me the *magician's patter* to make the illusion more convincing. He gave me a flyer of his wares to order by mail – it was everything I needed to launch my career.

By the time I graduated from high school I was presenting thirty-minute magic shows. New equipment was added to my act, the famous silver linking rings, the endless pouring water jar, the mysterious colored square, and the incredible shrinking rope. I presented parlor magic and entertained small groups

Making an Audience Disappear

at school, PTA meetings, and service clubs. Mr. Blackstone wasn't yet under threat, but I was gaining on him. First, however, I had to go to college.

I applied to the Student Entertainers Organization at Oklahoma A&M and was invited to try out. The director, Mr. Frank "Pappy" Martin judged my act to decide if I'd become an O-State Performer. He liked it and soon I was being sent around the campus and into the community to entertain. We were only paid $5 to $10 a gig, but it provided pocket money for a college freshman, and it was *showbiz*.

At some point, no matter how skilled or practiced, most run-of-the-mill magicians flub up an illusion. I bought a life-like stuffed skunk which I held inside my coat in case some bit didn't pan out. Then I'd let it fall to the floor while remarking, "Well, that was a stinker." It always brought laughs.

Toward the end of the spring semester I was assigned to a small rural school house some ten miles from the college. A community pot-luck dinner was the event and I was the entertainment. As I set up my equipment I noticed that many of the children were gathered right under my feet, looking up with expectation. Too close – as it would be easier to detect how some of my tricks were accomplished. But the room was small and the show must go on.

I opened my act with the disappearing scarf, followed by the linking rings illusion. About midway in my act all was going well – until I messed up. Time to drop the skunk for a laugh.

Country children know things that city kids don't. When the skunk hit the floor, pandemonium erupted.

Kids screamed and scrambled for the exits. Everyone thought it was the climax of the act, applauded, and began to leave.

Not long after that I decided I wouldn't be a magician.

Relax, Mr. Blackstone, relax.

ANGUISHED PROXIMITY

I crossed a railroad track and remembered
A sultry summer day long long ago
When my heart skipped a beat with hope

It was the summer of our lonely distance courtship
You still in high school, me headed for college
And few opportunities to see you.

My pastor encouraged me to do hard labor
You'll sit behind a desk much of your life
Mr. Morrow at Ready Mix Concrete hired me

Traveling in the non-air-conditioned truck
I rode in the cab, destination unknown
On State 51, I sat up, awake with expectation

We were headed toward Hennessey
Was it possible I might get to see you
But we turned south on a county road

All day we worked repairing a train trestle
And I mooned over your closeness,
Yet, the impossibility of reaching you

Today, I crossed that railroad track
And the memory came flooding back
Of anguished proximity, so long ago

THOSE HENNESSEY GIRLS

As with many lads in my hometown, I was recruited into a Cub Scout den around the age of eight. We met at the home of den mother, Mrs. Hunt. We did all those things Cub Scouts do, preparing for the day when we would become Boy Scouts. At twelve I joined the Troop that met at the Methodist Church. Mr. Benedict was the Scoutmaster, and was dedicated to making us all Eagle Scouts. I was to disappoint him.

Earning merit badges was key to rising from the rank of Tenderfoot to Second Class and ultimately to Eagle Scout. After two years I was still a Tenderfoot and, in spite of earnest coaching, unlikely to rise to Mr. Benedict's expectations. I think it was the knot-tying that did me in. I could never distinguish between a sheepshank and a bowline.

One Monday evening no one showed up for the scout meeting but me. I imagine I hadn't paid attention when Mr. Benedict announced they would not meet this week.

However, some kids from our church youth group were gathering. Sherry Kress, asked me if I was going with them to the District Youth Rally. I told her that I didn't know anything about it. She said: "Why don't you come along?"

It sounded like a good idea so I called and got permission from my mother.

The evening was exciting – singing, worship and food. And I wasn't asked to tie one knot. There was another advantage over the Boy Scouts ... girls. From then on church youth gatherings became my passion.

The presence of females was an enjoyable addition, especially a few girls from the little town of Hennessey. They were all pretty. Mostly, though, I noticed one– Paula Rue Carmony. With her beautiful green eyes, porcelain skin, and sweet smile she stood out from all the others.

In time we both became leaders in our sub-district and were together at rallies. I didn't think Paula noticed me, but I observed her – intently.

Our District was part of the West Oklahoma Annual Conference that sponsored a weeklong camp near Turner Falls in Southern Oklahoma. In this Arbuckle Mountain setting we learned about faith and met youths from across the western half of the state. Some have remained my lifelong friends.

Following graduation, I attended one more time because I had been elected the President the previous summer. Apparently, on the way to camp, Paula had been recruited to get me to date another girl from her town. Instead, I relished the attention Paula paid me, and soon her friend dropped out of our conversation. One day, as we stood under a scraggy pine tree at the edge of Honey Creek, I leaned over and kissed her. She didn't object. My heart was gone. At the end of the week we went back to our homes, but I began to write to her.

My pastor had urged me to take a job with the Murrow Ready Mix Concrete Company, and I returned from camp to a summer of hard labor. When I had asked him why I should leave my part time job selling clothes at J.C. Penney's, he said, "David, you'll spend your life working as a pastor, which is largely a desk job. You need to understand how working people live – spend time doing manual labor." I did, and it introduced me to a side of life I might never have known.

One day, after work, I arranged a ride with some friends who were going to a baseball game in Enid where Paula's sister lived. Paula would came up from Hennessey to meet me. But the afternoon I was to leave, my boss dropped a heavy jack on my foot. I was in no shape to travel, but wasn't about to miss the opportunity to see Paula. My ride let me off at her sister's house, and we walked the ten blocks downtown to see a movie. I limped all the way. My foot was so swollen by the time I got back to Perry that I couldn't report for work the next day. Ah, but it was worth it.

Fall arrived and I prepared to move to Stillwater to attend college, but convinced my parents to go by way of Hennessey to see Paula. That isn't a direct route, but then love never is. Our parents met, and I was off to school.

Later, on October 4th, I borrowed the folks' car and went to Hennessey where I picked up Paula and we drove to Enid to see Jerry Lewis and Dean

Martin in the movie *Jumping Jacks*. When we went back to the car, parked down a side street by a huge garbage can, in this least-of-all romantic settings, I proposed to Paula. *Would she marry me?* Her answer was a weak *yes*. Later, she said she wasn't sure I was serious. I was.

After a year at A&M I transferred to Oklahoma City University, our Methodist school. Paula graduated from high school and, thanks to their generous scholarship program, was able to join me at OCU.

We married on June 1, 1955 at First Methodist in Hennessey, her home church. Dr. Bonner Teeter, who had been the Dean of the camp at Turner Falls, performed the ceremony.

Those Hennessey girls were all so pretty. And I married the sweetest and prettiest of them all.

JESUS JUNKETS AND OTHER TRAVELS

MY PARENTS RARELY TOOK VACATIONS. There is one picture of me as a baby, being held by Dad in the Gulf of Mexico, an experience I was too young to remember. If the folks traveled, it was to visit my Aunt Eva and Uncle Jim. Once we visited them in St. Louis, where coal was the dominant heating fuel and soot blanketed everything. Other than the winter dark, all I remember was seeing the giant flying red horse symbol on the side of a building. The morning we left I looked out their dingy second story window at the street lamp's diffused light. It was good to return to the clean air of Oklahoma.

By the time I was twelve the war had ended and Grandmother Mossman took me on a long train-bus trip to Louisiana to visit my aunt and uncle. Other than those few events, my worldly travels were non-existent.

Before retirement I had the privilege of going on many of what my colleagues called *Jesus Junkets*. From 1963 to 2012, I was an observer, an elected delegate, or an officer of all but two General or

Jurisdictional Conferences of the United Methodist Church. I served on the General Council on Ministries of our church for eight years which afforded me travel to Germany, Norway, Mexico and The Philippines.

As the Annual Conference Mission Secretary, I was part of a group visiting Haiti. The abject poverty of that country was like nothing I had ever seen. Another trip was to Africa where we traversed the continent observing the work of our church in Liberia, Kenya, Zimbabwe and Mozambique. In Kenya we crossed the equator and I was surprised to see wheat growing there just like back home in Oklahoma.

In 1953 at Oklahoma City University, Paula and I were active in the Independent Student Association. The ISA provided fellowship and a venue for seeking leadership in student governance.

The ISA grew – challenged and won student offices, and became a viable campus presence. I was elected Vice-president of the Student Body.

ISA decided to send a delegation to the national meeting of Independent Students in Fort Collins, Colorado. Four were selected, Marvin Nelson, Margaret Harris, Paula and me. An assistant librarian, Ruth Cox, who could not have been more than a few years older, was sent as our chaperone.

Marvin served a weekend church in Berlin on the west side of the state. I was assigned to the church at Harrah, east of Oklahoma City. Margaret and Paula and Ruth worked together in the University library.

The plan was for me to preach on Sunday morning, go by OCU and pick up Paula, Margaret, and Ruth, in my older vehicle, and drive to Berlin.

We piled into Marvin's new car and drove all night to Ft. Collins, Colorado. We arrived about five in the morning to a town shut tight. The dorm wasn't available until ten a.m. and no open cafés could be found. We settled down to sleep in the car.

We awoke at daylight to falling snow. From the windless sky the white flakes piled high on strands of wire. By mid-afternoon it stopped, leaving two feet of drift and the world a wonderland.

That evening, we were invited to join a gathering of students for fellowship at an address on the edge of town. When we arrived we realized the place was a bar.

Marvin, who was still in his extreme conservative religious stage, refused to go in where liquor was being served. We sat in the car trying to figure out what to do. For some crazy reason, we decided to drive north to Cheyenne, Wyoming, almost fifty miles away, to have dinner. Out on the road we followed the snow plow, now and then noticing cars stalled in snow banks. We arrived, and later, when we saw newspaper stories – realized how dangerous our trip had been.

The following day we followed a road that led to a city park. The sun was shining and we enjoyed the warmth, even though the temperature was in the lower teens. We threw snowballs and climbed a large boulder in the middle of a snowfield to take pictures.

A day or so later we were in a drugstore purchasing picture postcards to send to our friends. One was from that city park, taken in summer time, and we realized that the large rock we had climbed was in the middle of a lake. We could have broken through the ice and plunged to certain death. Our first travel excursion might well have been our last. We did not tell our kids this story when they were growing up.

The experience of travel was an education itself. Learning about cultures different than mine, meeting people with backgrounds and understandings so unlike my own, provided me with a broad perspective and a deep joy of our human family. I became a member of the whole world.

After retirement from the Annual Conference in 2005 until 2016 I served as the Executive Director of the South Central Jurisdiction. Travels associated with that position took me all over the southwest.

For a lad who listened to the distant whistle of passing trains in the night and wondered if I would ever see the world beyond Noble County, I did well.

SIX MILE SUNRISE

Flying six miles above the earth,
I watched the world slowly awaken,
Like a late reveler the morning after,
Feebly grasping to hold one last dream,
Red-eyed, unfocused, stirring from slumber.

Shadows dissolved before advancing light.
Purple peaks stretched up to catch first shafts.
Deep valleys asleep sullen and gray.
Dotted lakes flashed staccato bursts of sheen,
As if text-messaging the new day aborning.

A silver winding river sent up wisps of fog.
Tiny fingers held up to test the wind's direction.
Stars faded with one last wink in shimmering sky.
The plane slid into the brown smog of Houston,
Leaving behind the awe and wonder of daybreak.

MOTIVATION

STUDENT PASTORS ARE A SPECIAL BREED. Unable to afford a full-time clergy, small congregations are assigned preachers-to-be while they are in college or seminary.

The spirit of these congregations is, "We get to grow up another preacher."

These wonderful people endure unpolished sermons and put up with erratic schedules in order to have a minister. In return they offer their inexperienced pastor *on-the-job training*, and teach them important lessons, some not covered by institutions of higher learning.

My first student appointment was seventy-five miles from the university. I preached Sunday mornings and evenings, met with the youth, conducted meetings, visited the sick, and buried the dead. Morning worship attendance averaged fifty, but only ten to twelve came to the evening service.

My 1937 Buick, in its sixteenth year, was untrustworthy for the round trip between school and church. So, I rode the bus, leaving my car at my parents' home fifteen miles from the community where I served. Because the evening service was too late for me to catch the six-thirty bus I had to take the eleven-p.m. run, arriving at school after midnight.

The evening service seemed such a waste of time. Those few worshipers were the saints of the church. I reasoned they only came out of habit. So, one Sunday morning I announced the evening worship was discontinued. I would meet with the youth early and be on the six-thirty bus. The announcement was met with stony silence, which I mistakenly perceived to be indifference, or relief. By eight-thirty that evening I was back on campus. This new arrangement pleased me, and it meant I could see Paula before her 10:30 p.m. curfew. It was not to be that simple.

On Wednesday, my District Superintendent contacted me. He said the leaders of the church had called him saying they'd decided that if I wouldn't hold the Sunday evening service, they would find somebody who would, and subtract the cost from my salary. He guessed it would be about ten dollars a week. Since I was only getting $150 a month I felt a surge of new enthusiasm for Sunday evening worship. The next week I was on the 11:00 p.m. bus back to school.

But motivation worked both ways.

The following year I was appointed to Harrah, twenty-five miles from the school, a wonderful improvement. Now Paula, whom I would marry the next summer, could ride out to the church with me. And it paid $200 more a year.

Upon arrival I discovered they were building a new sanctuary and education wing. The project was finished to the top of the windows but there were no funds for a roof. Winter was not far away.

Resources were sought all over the area without success. A mini-recession was gripping the country and, even in good times, banks are reluctant to make loans to churches. Ultimately a local church family loaned the money and we had a roof before cold weather.

Much of the labor on the building was done by the members and steady but slow progress was made until time to paint the inside walls of the sanctuary. Volunteer weariness set in.

A wedding for one of the more prominent families of the congregation had been scheduled at a time when we were sure the building would be finished. As that date loomed, the walls remained unpainted. Floors could not be finished or pews set until that task was done. It was not the setting that the bride or her mother expected for what they envisioned as *the* community's wedding of the year.

An idea popped into my head. We were already using the unfinished sanctuary for worship. Saturday evening, I drove to the church, opened a can of paint and drew large rectangles on the bare walls. In each one I lettered the name of a family of the congregation.

When folks arrived the next day, they saw their names framed in large letters on the walls of the sanctuary. I explained that the church would be open every day that week and all they had to do was come by and paint out the panel with their name in it.

There was a moment of awkward silence in which I wasn't sure I would get away with my plan . . . then someone laughed, and the congregation exploded in

Motivation

glee and applause. A new energy to finish the work blossomed. The painting was all done within the week. The carpet and pews were installed in time for the wedding. The bride was beautiful, and happy.

So was her mother.

THE ART OF CLEANING CESSPOOLS

I WAS EIGHTEEN AND THE NEWLY ASSIGNED student pastor of First Methodist Morrison, a church that had run off its last two preachers. I had one sermon, preached twice. I'd never led an entire worship service, conducted a funeral, baptized anyone, or performed a wedding.

The church was fifteen miles from my hometown in a small community of eight hundred people. After my first year in college, my home pastor, Howard Bush, arranged my assignment there. I knew he would coach me in my first outing as a pastor. I expected, if necessary, he'd help pick up the pieces.

Unfortunately, that year he was moved to a church five hundred miles away. So, besides my lack of experience, my mentor now lived in another state.

It is true that fools rush in where angels fear to tread. I was confident I would succeed when older more experienced pastors had failed.

Two leading families nursed a smoldering feud that divided the congregation. Few remembered what started it, but where you sat in the sanctuary was a declaration of loyalty to one or the other faction. The only time they agreed was when they decided the pastor should be moved. Several years after I left, lightning struck and burned the church. It surprised me it hadn't happened at eleven on a Sunday morning.

My decision not to live in their dilapidated parsonage next to the church may have been a mistake. Uneven, creaky floors hinted one might fall through. Wallpaper hung in loose strips and the permeating smell was musty. From the maroon sofa, with excelsior poking out, to the stained lumpy mattress, it appeared more a storehouse for old furniture.

Choosing to live at home, the congregation was probably relieved. They wouldn't have to fix it up. Later, I realized they had no intention of spending a dime on it. It was good enough for the minister, especially an unmarried one.

The good folks muttered about my not moving in. When concerns were expressed about the pastor, they began with some other complaint and ended, ". . . and he refuses to live in our parsonage."

With no bathroom in the church building it was necessary to use the parsonage facilities. Small towns were usually on septic systems with drain pipes from the house to a concrete or metal tank buried at the back of a property. Sewage flowed in, liquids evaporated, solids didn't. In time it had to be pumped out.

That summer, following the Vacation Bible School, the tank was full causing sewage to back up into the bathtub when the toilet was flushed. It was time to inform the Official Board at the next meeting.

Someone would move that the Trustees be authorized to see to it, and it would be done.

There must be an unwritten rule which states: *A problem will take time inversely proportional to the simplicity of the decision required.*

I presented the need. Silence followed. Someone opened with, "I thought we cleaned that out not long ago." The discussion continued in a ping pong fashion with everyone generally agreeing that it was *jest a while back*.

Meanwhile Mary Grace Appleton, the secretary, was digging in her official filing cabinet, an old purse. She pulled a faded sheet of paper from its deep recesses and said, "Here it is. Two years ago, on April 8th, we paid Timmons Septic $15 for cleaning services."

Another silence signals round two – *we could probably get some fellers together and do it ourselves and save money*. This takes considerable time as they discuss who has the right equipment and hired hands.

By rights the Trustees should take responsibility, but their chair isn't here tonight, and will not know anything about the discussion as nobody will tell him. A month can go by with nothing done. Meanwhile the parsonage is getting deeper in the backwash of the cesspool.

At this point the pastor may try either of two things. One, he can call the septic cleaning people and order the work done, and present the bill at the next Board meeting.

This is a commando tactic – guaranteed to backfire. Much clamor will descend upon the preacher's head. He will be told that he had no business committing the church to what may be an unnecessary expense and, if he ever does it again, there will be the dickens to pay. It would be embarrassing to answer the query: "Why did you leave your last church" with, "Unauthorized cleaning of cesspool."

The second method is more subtle. No announcement is made about the septic. Instead, the pastor invites the church ladies to an afternoon tea at the parsonage. A warm day is the optimum setting. Let the cesspool do the talking.

"Odor? Yes, I guess it is a little strong today . . . care for another cookie?"

No Board meeting will be needed, no committee assigned. The next morning the septic tank company will arrive at eight sharp.

Being inexperienced in such matters, I was stunned when Frank, one of the leading laymen said, "Well, these new-fangled things never did work. We need to go out back and dig two holes and put up an outhouse." What really got me in trouble was that I laughed out loud. He was dead serious.

Thankfully, there are those in every congregation who get things done. In a meeting they may not say much and they won't argue over methods. But in a day or two they appear at the parsonage with the proper equipment, fix the problem and are gone. The only thanks they desire is that the pastor and family be quietly grateful, and attentive to the tasks of ministry.

For these blessed few every pastor gives heartfelt thanks.

AN ANGEL IN KHAKI

THE YEAR ENDED AT MORRISON, AND I requested an assignment closer to Oklahoma City University. So, in 1953 I was sent to Harrah, a small community twenty miles east of the city.

My predecessor, Lawrence Grubb, also a student pastor, had invited Civil Rights Activist, Ms. Clara Luper, to speak at the church one Sunday evening. Larry was highly thought of, but his brave appeal on an unpopular social issue led some to believe it was the reason he was moved. In reality it wasn't, but that rumor persisted after I arrived.

In those days, to receive reports on the life of the congregation, the District Superintendent held a Quarterly Conference at each church. When I announced that Dr. Clegg would be visiting, Clara Seigfried jumped up, "Well, when he gets here I'll give him a piece of my mind for moving Larry!"

Caution not being a ready trait of mine, I fired back: "Clara, maybe you should stay home that day!"

Those who were upset over Larry's move took a while to accept me as their pastor. But we had to focus on finishing construction of a new sanctuary and education wing. Membership had outgrown the small frame building. The new building was in progress, but the congregation was financially strapped. The leadership, with memories of the Great Depression, was reluctant to incur debt.

The State highway angled through town creating odd-shaped lots. The church sat on a triangle of ground facing a city street. Several residences, all bordered the highway on the north. They moved the old sanctuary to the back of the lot and began the new building.

The congregation provided most of the labor and the project had taken considerable time. The summer I arrived, construction had halted at the top of the windows. By fall, with winter coming, no progress had been made. Reluctantly the Trustees agreed to borrow $10,000 to install the roof and complete the building.

The mini-recession of the mid 1950s made it tough to borrow money. No bank would make us a loan. As one banker put it, "It's too risky, and besides, we'd look bad if we had to foreclose on a church."

Part of my tuition at Oklahoma City University was provided by a Broadhurst Scholarship for ministerial students. Mr. Broadhurst, a banker and philanthropist, officed in a skyscraper in downtown Tulsa. I made an appointment to see him, hoping he might agree to a loan.

Taking the elevator to the top floor and entering the richly paneled complex was intimidating. After a long wait I was ushered into an even more ornate office. My hoped-for benefactor peered down from his enormous desk and inquired why I was there.

I thanked him for my scholarship and told of the plight of our church trying to finish its building. I shared financials with him to show we could repay the debt, but he seemed more interested in the spirit of the congregation. Later, I realized he was asking questions to determine if I was theologically conservative enough to suit him. He said he would consider the matter and call me in a few days.

When the call came, Mr. Broadhurst agreed but at 6% interest, double the going rate. But with time running out and no other options in sight, the Trustees met to consider his offer.

As we deliberated there came a soft knock at the door. It was Carl Onsman, the owner of the gas station next door. He was a small graying man in his early sixties. He and his wife rarely missed worship. Sundays he donned freshly starched khakis, which I suspect he wore the rest of the week.

The puzzled Trustees greeted him warmly.

He spoke with a quiet voice, "I understand you've run into some trouble borrowing money to finish the building. Mrs. Onsman and I have talked it over and we'd like to loan the church the $10,000. If you could pay us back at 3% interest it'd be okay with us."

The stunned Trustees quickly agreed and soon the church had a roof and was winterized.

Student pastors had been assigned there for many years with the expectation they would live on campus. Two years later, when I graduated from college and headed for seminary, the church decided to ask for a full-time minister. I was their last student.

They would need a parsonage. Again, the Onsmans came through with a loan for a house.

Truly he was an angel in khakis.

MR. BUCK

MY HOME TOWN PASTOR AND MENTOR advised me to keep a student appointment in Oklahoma while attending graduate school in Dallas. He said I would *maintain awareness by the powers-that-be-in-the-conference,* and, after graduation, they would know me better than students who were out of sight for those years. So, I was appointed to the Springer Methodist Church, north of Ardmore, a hundred and twenty miles from Perkins School of Theology at SMU.

The Springer church ran a food booth at the Carter county fair, serving lunch and dinner for workers and attendees. No restaurants were within a mile of the fairgrounds. Proceeds helped pay their missional commitments.

I came up with a great idea to increase the income. Since carnival workers and high school Future Farmers of America (FFA) kids slept nights at the fairgrounds why didn't we serve breakfasts?

The response to my brilliance was less than positive. The loyal but weary Fair Food Team calculated that adding breakfasts, while making more money, meant more work. The Board's reaction was to sing a verse of that famous hymn of the Church Reluctant: *We Never Did It That Way Before*. This is performed as a chorus with solo parts, occasional duets, and always in a minor key.

Seasoned members have rules for volunteers, "Those who propose something new can jolly-well do the labor." The second rule is, "If you keep your mouth shut, you might kill any new idea."

Later in my career I learned more acceptable ways to present new dreams, but I occasionally made those off-the-wall suggestions in meetings. It wakes those who doze.

As my proposal was about to die for lack of a second, and the crowd was beginning to relax, Mr. Buchanan spoke up: "If the preacher will do the cooking, I'll go help him."

Mr. Buck was at least 80 years old. A life of hard labor had left his hands gnarled and drawn, his right hand missing most of his pointing finger, and his frame shrunken to a stooped five feet. Working outdoors, rain or shine, had crinkled his skin, and his nearly bald head was pocked where the surgeon had cut out numerous skin cancers.

I had moved into the parsonage in June to discover the water well was dry. Paula was eight months pregnant with our first child and staying with her parents in Hennessy. Mr. Buck volunteered to help drill the new well to have sweet clear water when Paula and our new baby, Sherri, came home later that summer.

The board promptly agreed to my serving breakfast suggestion. So, a young, inexperienced minister and a crusty old saint showed up bright and early on that first morning of the Carter County Free Fair, eager to feed the multitudes. Carnies and sleepy-eyed youths made grateful customers.

In the annals of sainthood, Mr. Buck probably will not be listed as a biblical scholar, a competent theologian, or a notable contributor to the faith. But his kind never stops believing that something new might take place in this tired old world. We did, in fact, raise more funds than ever.

I sought out these holy servants in every congregation I served. They were great counsel, and creative, willing accomplices, who refused to sing "We Never Did It That Way Before."

Praise God from whom all blessings flow.

SAY, SON, YOU TOO PROUD TO LEARN SOMETHING?

CHURCH FOLKS PREPARE TASTY FARE FOR church dinners, bake sales, and bazaars. Some have specialty dishes. Everyone honors Connie Jones for her pickled beets. No one brings that dish unless they ever intended to challenge her and Mrs. Wallace will firmly inform the upstart that hers are good, but "don't come a country mile close to the County Free Fair Champion beet-pickler, Mrs. Connie Jones, thank you very much."

Virtually every dish served at a church dinner is some lady's *piece de résistance*. Rolls, that would be Beth Kaiser's double raised, twice buttered, clover leafs. Sally Adam's candied yams with toasted pecans are to die for. And no feast would be complete without Lucy Johnson's Dutch apple pie. And if you're number nine in the serving line, don't hope to get a slice.

My father was an excellent cook. A bachelor for years he learned to feed himself. When he and Mom married she had no idea how to prepare a meal. He taught her and she became a great cook. He was noted for feeding large numbers of people at community gatherings, lodge dinners and sportsmen's events. His barbecue sauce was popular as well as his secret-ingredient chili. So the idea of a man in the kitchen was not new to me. I love to cook, and Paula and I often share in preparing meals. It is not, however, a skill required of the clergy.

At the church in Springer I served full time in the summer and, during school, commuted weekends from the seminary.

As fall approached the church planned the annual fund raiser, a food booth at the Carter County Free Fair. This year, for the first time, Mr. Buck and I were commissioned to serve breakfasts.

I'd never prepared food on an outdoor propane-heated grill. Nor was I skilled at producing multiple meals simultaneously. Quickly our booth filled with hungry people. The first orders were a shipwreck. The eggs were overcooked, the bacon burned, and the pancakes . . . ugly, gooey and stuck to the grill.

As I struggled, a voice behind me called out, "Say, son, you too proud to learn something?"

I turned to see one of the carnies – a man whose rugged features and deep tan resulted from years of outdoor labor. Perched on a stool he let his question hang in the air as he glanced at me, the growing mess on the grill, then back at me.

"No, sir," I said. "What do you suggest?"

"Can I show you?"

I handed him my spatula, and waved him inside. He ducked under the counter, turned down the heat and removed all the inedible food from the grill. He found a pumice stone and scraped away the greasy residue. Putting a few drops of oil on a cloth he polished the surface until it gleamed like a black pearl. A sprinkle of water on the griddle sizzled and instantly vaporized. He turned the fire down and tried again. When the drops danced a few seconds before turning to steam, he pronounced it just right.

Adding oil and a measure of sugar to the pancake batter, he poured several puddles on the grill and began frying bacon and eggs. In no time the cakes began to bubble. When he deftly turned them, they were golden brown and didn't stick.

As I watched this miracle he explained the importance of keeping the grill clean and lightly lubricated. The oil in the batter would prevent the pancakes from sticking.

"The sugar," he said "gives them the color."

With a flick of his wrist he turned the eggs, dished up a meal and served it to a customer, handed me the spatula, and slipped back under the counter. The customers applauded. Mr. Buck and I were so impressed that we awarded him free breakfasts every morning during the fair. He accepted and all week offered more suggestions to improve my short order skills.

I shudder to think how it might have turned out had I been too proud to learn something new.

MY SEMINARY DAZE

DEAN MERRIMAN CUNNINGHAM, FOLLOWED by the seminary faculty, strode purposefully down the center aisle of the auditorium as the incoming class of 1956 grew quiet. He surveyed the hundred or so eager faces, mostly men, who gathered for the orientation of what would be the Class of '59. We were beginning a three-year journey. All of us planned to be preachers, missionaries, seminary teachers, Christian educators or ministers of music.

The Dean welcomed us and introduced the members of the faculty who would have the task of forming us into credible theologians and knowledgeable pastors. He peered over his dark-rimmed glasses perched at the end of his nose, eyes sweeping the room, "How many of you majored in religion in undergraduate school?" Many hands went up. "Well, while you are here you will need to unlearn much of what you were taught. You arrived here with a faith largely given to you by parents, preachers and teachers. In three years, you will leave with a faith you own, if you stay."

In undergraduate school I had majored in psychology, but had taken most of the religion courses offered at Oklahoma City University. I contemplated what I needed to unlearn from Drs. McGee, and Hanson.

The Dean said we would take core courses in the first year in New Testament, Old Testament, and Church History. The middler year we would have homiletics, the art and practice of preaching, pastoral care, and Methodist polity and governance. The final year we would be immersed in systematic theology, and write our credo – a coherent statement of our theological understanding of faith. It would be graded by one of the three major professors in that field – Dr. Albert Outler, acclaimed Wesleyan theologian, Dr. John Deschner, or Dr. Schubert Ogden, the newest addition to the systematics faculty. Advanced electives were available in all core subjects as we progressed through the three years.

Classes were Tuesday through Friday. None on Mondays as some held student appointments on the weekend and needed Monday to return to campus. Chapel was on Tuesdays and Thursdays. Attendance was expected, but not required.

Cunningham's closing remark was ominous, "I will tell you now that not all of you will graduate. Some will drop out, some will transfer elsewhere, and some of you we will flunk. Good luck."

Dr. Cunningham was of the conviction that seminary was primarily for gifted students to go on and get their Ph.Ds. and teach. If you were not *bright enough* to do that well, there was always the local church ministry. I planned to return to Oklahoma and be a pastor. Cunningham was not impressed.

Fortunately, at the end of my first year he left and a new dean arrived.

Dean Dr. Joe Quillian was a true gentleman of the south, with a honeyed Georgia accent and amid his salt and pepper coif a shock of white hair for dignity. He taught homiletics and instructed us on an elaborate outline for writing sermons, and insisted we preach without notes. However, when he preached in chapel, he used a legal yellow pad – turning each page as he spoke, letting it hang over the edge of the pulpit. *Do as I say, not as I do?*

In homiletics we prepared and preached sermons that were recorded on camera so Dean Quillian could review and analyze our style and content. When my turn came, he asked me afterward which preacher I was patterning my delivery.

I said I wasn't copying anyone.

He said, "You sound like the TV minister at Draper Street Christian Church."

Having never heard that preacher, I protested.

He insisted that I had seen him on television at some point and was unconsciously imitating him. It wasn't true but I realized I did sound like my mentor-pastor back home. Like writers, a preacher must find his own voice. This takes time, even years.

Every professor acted as though his class was the only one in which you were enrolled. The collective reading assignments could easily be 500 pages daily. Not easy when I worked from 3:30 to 11:00 p.m. each day. And you never knew when a prof would open class by saying, "Take out a piece of paper, I have a pop quiz for you."

Each had their own style. Our Old Testament teacher was a refugee from a World War II German concentration camp. He spoke with a thick accent, and struggled to keep his composure – dealing with lingering issues from that experience. Often, passing his door in the afternoons, we could hear him ranting and wailing in the depths of his office.

Dr. Ritchie Hogg taught church history. His delivery was so machine-gun fast it was said that, if you dropped your pencil during a lecture, by the time you picked it up you would have missed two hundred years of church history.

The majority of professors held Ph.Ds. but the course on Methodist polity and governance was taught by a former District Superintendent, Dr. Marvin Judy, who knew that field better than the theologians.

Following Chapel one day, where the North Texas College Jazz group had performed a poignant jazz requiem in memory of the death of a young girl, we gathered in Dr. Judy's class.

He was extremely upset over what he considered to be inappropriate music in worship. Red-faced, he held forth for several minutes on his reaction to the event, ending with the statement, "I just don't see why they have to play whorehouse music in church."

In the short silence, a voice from the back of the room said, "How did you know, Dr. Judy, how did you know?"

In college, if I received a less than satisfactory grade I usually went to talk to the professor. It sometimes increased my grade by a point or two.

Midway through my courses I took a summer class on the Gospel of John, from Dr. Wesley Davis. He was a mild-mannered sweet man in his mid-sixties, whose lectures were soft voiced as he rocked back and forth, heel to toe. I did not do well in the class and received an F on my final. So I thought I would pay him a visit, believing I could get my grade up to at least a D.

He welcomed me into his tiny book-lined office, and listened as I gave him my best spiel on how I had to hold a job to stay in school, and all my excellent reasons why the grade should be higher. After I finished, he looked at the ceiling for a few moments, then said to me, "Now, brother Severe, I think we both know that is the grade you earned."

I was shocked, but it became a turning point. That fall I was determined to acquire knowledge. I studied with a new intensity. The promised transformation to a *faith owned* began to materialize. I acquired skills that would make me a life-long learner.

The final year of seminary is a concentration on systematic theology. Mondays, Wednesdays and Fridays we listened, in rotation, to lectures by the three professors in that discipline. On Tuesdays and Thursdays, we were divided into three groups and assigned to one of them for an intensive three-hour colloquy. All our theologians were considered formidable, but the most feared was Dr. Schubert Ogden.

"Welcome to my colloquy, gentlemen. My name is Schubert Ogden. I am a graduate of The University of Chicago, and finishing my dissertation for a Ph.D. from Phillips-Universitat in Marburg, Germany. I am a Process Theologian, more about which you will learn as we go through this semester. I grade on a ten-point system. Ten is perfect and only God is perfect, so don't get your hopes up."

We wondered if we had any hope at all. We also realized that he was barely six years our senior. Most professors were considerably older. But there was no doubt about Ogden's being in command.

A colloquy is, by definition, a discussion, but in his class it was a lecture, interrupted by his sudden stopping and turning to one of us. *Mr. Severe, please elaborate on what I have just said.* Then I had to defend my response against his push-back questions. It was terrifying, but taught us to pay attention, think on our feet and, stand up for our beliefs.

Writing our credo – our personal, rational statement of what we believed, was the final hurdle to graduation. Mine would be graded by Dr. Ogden. This led to weeks of research, days and nights of writing and on the appointed day, inside a neatly lettered folder, I turned it in with fear and trembling. It was only weeks until the end of the semester. If I passed, I graduated. If I didn't – it meant another semester and repeating systematic theology.

When my credo was handed back, I opened the folder, afraid to see my grade. On the front page, in the top left corner was 8.5. In Ogden's grading method it was the equivalent of a B+. I would graduate.

Dr. Davis, I am forever grateful.

THE PROJECT

REMEMBER HIGH FIDELITY RECORDS? They were an improvement over the scratchy long playing 78 rpm platters that reigned until the 1950s. But new hi-fi equipment was required to play them. Old mono-platters became as out of date as spats.

By the late-fifties the *in* thing was to purchase a Hi-Fi tuner, speakers and turntable as separate parts. Previously, these components had been tucked inside shiny veneer cabinets. Now they perched on your bookshelves. One speaker placed to the right of the receiver, the other an equal distance to the left. Listening in the middle gave you the richness of true high fidelity. It was the latest fad, and I wanted it.

Such exotic equipment was well beyond the budget of a seminary student in their first year of grad school and married with a baby. Somehow, we found the money to purchase an inexpensive set, and a couple of new hi-fi albums.

Among them was Antol Diorite's *1812 Overture* in which cannon fire had been recorded, and rerecorded, until it created a formidable blast. Following the overture, a bonus track explained how they made the cannon shots.

The Project

We enjoyed the music in our small apartment, a dorm apartment for married students, with tile floors, and lathe and plaster walls and ceilings. The place was a sound chamber.

In exchange for free housing in each dorm, the University employed one of the seminarians as a resident director to oversee the building. I applied but the job went to a student from a well-to-do family. He had never struggled financially and that didn't go well with others who had applied who, like us, were financially strapped. The new director had a haughty attitude which increased our resentment. A mischievous plot occurred to me.

Late one night, I cracked opened our apartment door and set one of my new speakers in the hallway. Then, placing the needle directly on the cannon shot, I turned the volume full blast. The combination of the high fidelity and the building's floors and walls hard surfaces created a resounding explosion. I pulled the speaker back, closed the door and waited. Three doors down, the resident director burst out of his apartment. I jerked open my door, ran into the hall, looking wildly, and yelled, "*What was that?*"

He ordered me back inside as he searched the boiler and equipment rooms, and the trash dump. He couldn't figure it out, but didn't report the incident. Several nights later, I repeated the ruse. He went through the routine, to no avail. After the third time, I tired of the game. He never knew what went boom in the night.

Following graduation, I decided to build a cabinet for my hi-fi equipment. Birch would be excellent material. The Hydro lumberyard would be glad to order it. Fifty dollars was a lot of money but we would have a handsome piece to admire.

Paula was not convinced this was a bright idea. I assured her that I had taken shop in high school, and a well-educated person with two degrees should be able to figure out a simple wooden music cabinet. I placed the order.

I had only hand tools. I possessed a handsaw, a T-square, hammer, screwdriver, pliers, and two C-clamps which I never figured how to use.

Though I had no blueprint, I worked with diligence, picturing the finished creation. It would be such a pleasure to say to guests, "Would you like to hear my hi-fi? I built the cabinet."

The project was more difficult than I imagined. I remembered, from high school, how hard it had been to square a pine block, a requirement before you were allowed to use power equipment.

I also recalled another class project. I'd wanted to make my mom a deep walnut bowl for pecans, with a center riser to hold picks. This involved using the wood lathe, an exciting but daunting piece of equipment. In my mind I could see the polished bowl sitting on the dining room table, mother pointing to it proudly and saying to her friends, "See that . . . David made it."

However, each time I got the lip of the bowl almost right, I gouged a deep gash and had to trim the edge to match. Once, the whole thing flew off the lathe, and went clattering about the shop. This chipped another deep cut in the rim and knocked out

The Project

the centerpiece. I whittled on it until only an inch-deep dish was left. Still, I thought it was handsome. Mother used it, but I don't recall her mentioning to any of her friends that I had made it.

Undaunted, I finished the hi-fi cabinet. It leaned and wobbled because no corner was square. It resembled something created by Picasso or Dali. Our daughter ran her tricycle into it and the whole thing collapsed.

What I salvaged from the fifty dollars' worth of fine birch and hours of labor was a flat piece of wood eighteen inches square. I bolted the Christmas tree stand to it and it lasted several years. Though it was covered with a decorative skirt, I often pointed out to interested friends that I had built the base.

"Yes sir. . .I did it with hand tools, a keen eye, and a couple of C-clamps!"

UNINTENDED CONSEQUENCES

SEMINARY GRADUATION WAS SIX MONTHS away when an unexpected phone call brought a mixed blessing.

"Hello, this is Dr. Dwight Hunt, from the Clinton District in Oklahoma. Is this David?"

"Yes, sir, how are you?"

"I'm just fine. Bishop Smith asked me to call you and offer you the church at Hydro starting in January, 1959. Would you be interested?"

"Well, sir, I still have a semester of school. Is the Bishop suggesting I not finish?"

"No, no, Bishop Smith wants you to graduate, but thought you might be willing to commute to the church on weekends, then stay-on full time after school. There is a parsonage where your family could live. The salary is $2,400 a year."

I knew enough about the process to understand that the bishop's emissary was not suggesting I think it over for a few days. I asked for a half-hour to talk with Paula, and I would call him back.

"Well, we are in a Cabinet meeting right now and need to know. Can you make it fifteen minutes?"

"Yes, sir, fifteen minutes."

A flurry of conversation followed –

How far is it from Dallas? Get the map. Wow! Two hundred and fifty-seven miles.

Salary not much. But $300 a year better than I was being paid as a clerk for the Dallas Police Department. We didn't realize that gasoline costs would more than eat up that amount.

My 1948 Buick couldn't possibly hold up to that commute. Could we buy a better one? We would start looking.

Sherri was two and a half and Artie nine months – we would have to leave their pediatricians. Would there be doctors in Hydro? Probably not.

Where could I stay during the week in Dallas? No clue.

As the minutes ticked away, there was little doubt that I wanted to say yes. I was ready and less sensitive to Paula's concern of being alone with the kids all week. She assented and I called the District Superintendent and accepted.

We stuffed our meager belongings into the new car –an inexpensive bright red 1955 Studebaker Conestoga station wagon. It had no radio or air-conditioner. We arrived in a snow storm the week after Christmas 1959.

I found an upstairs bedroom to rent from one of the seminary professors in Dallas. There followed a long six months of leaving the campus on Thursdays around five p.m. and arriving in Hydro after ten, having sung every hymn and show tune I could think of to keep me awake. Then, on Monday afternoon following a weekend of pastoral duties, I headed back to Dallas.

And the unintended consequences? I had conducted few funerals in my young career but, in all of them, I had ridden to the cemetery with the funeral director in the hearse.

In Hydro that was not the custom. Here the minister was expected to lead the procession from the church to the grave – in his own car. The assistant took my keys and parked my car in front of the black hearse. That year each funeral procession, from the Methodist Church, was led, not by a dignified colored vehicle – but by a bright red Studebaker Conestoga station wagon.

Talk about going out in style.

COMFORT YE MY PEOPLE

As I began my post seminary ministry at age twenty-four, I reflected on my first student appointment. I was eighteen then, a college sophomore. The church was in Morrison, a community of eight hundred people. On a bright June Sunday morning in 1953, I conducted my first worship service and preached the only sermon I'd ever written. Now, after almost three years of seminary, and student pastorates at Harrah and Springer, I was beginning as pastor in Hydro, a community of eighteen hundred.

My sermon that first Sunday in Morrison had been warmly received. Thankfully folks are kind to fledgling ministers. I greeted my new parishioners, after church, and began putting names and faces together.

As the crowd dwindled, one man waited – signaling he needed a more private conversation. Ray, the Lay Leader of the church, a liaison officer between the pastor and the congregation, welcomed me and visited a few minutes, then said, "By the way, you need to make two home visits this afternoon. Two members have died and the families are counting on you to do their funerals. The first is Tuesday morning and the second Thursday afternoon."

Until then I'd attended one funeral, read the scripture at another, and been a pallbearer in a third. None of the deceased had been family members. I had no personal experience with grief or conducting an entire service.

That afternoon I called on the two families – clueless as to what I needed to say or ask. I'm sure they were aware of my nervousness, and inexperience. Thankfully they were eager to tell me about their loved ones and I came away with a basic understanding of their lives.

Having one funeral my first week was daunting ... how would I manage a second? Monday, I drove to a neighboring community and the Poteet mortuary that would handle both burials. Confessing my lack of experience, I threw myself on the mercy of the funeral director. Compassionate and encouraging, he explained the usual service and the minister's role and assured me that he'd be there for me. Each service went reasonably well. Nobody mentioned my anxiety.

In the decades since that shaky beginning, I consider conducting comforting funerals one of my best skills. A pastor may be forgiven if his sermons are not always gems, but you won't *wear well* if unable to comfort people in times of grief.

In those early days I thought I should be able to explain death. But there are no words with which do that. But, I learned to offer presence ... care ... warmth ... humor, and the compassion to weep with those who suffered loss. It eases a family's anxiety to share life events and humorous stories about their departed. Retelling these as part of the funeral brings solace.

I arrived in Hydro with several years of experience in conducting this most sacred rite.

George Meacham, our Sunday School Superintendent, was a dairyman and wheat farmer. Following classes, we gathered in the sanctuary, celebrated birthdays and anniversaries and listened to George's closing devotional. A gifted speaker, his stories were often better preaching than I was about to deliver. He and his wife Pat became great friends to Paula and me.

However, one practice of this community upset me – the inviting of former pastors to conduct funerals. In our tradition we are not to return and perform such rites and if requested –are to politely refuse. The resident minister should be granted the opportunity to care for the congregation. On rare occasions there are exceptions, but only at the invitation of the current clergy. A few former pastors habitually ignored this rule. Consequently, in eighteen months, I preached fewer than half of the funerals. I tried to be gracious each time, but quietly seethed.

When it came time to move, my last Sunday, I thanked the congregation for their kindness to me and my family, and stated that, as is our Methodist custom, they should not expect me to return to perform pastoral functions, specifically funerals.

After church, as people bade us goodbye, George waited outside, his face red with anger. When I approached him he shouted at me, "So, you won't come do my funeral? I thought we were good friends!"

I said, "I hope I will always be your friend George, but no I won't. Whoever is your pastor at that time should do it. If you like I'll come and sit with Pat and the kids but I won't preach your funeral."

More than forty years later, word came to me that George had died. He often served as a lay speaker and had been invited to fill the pulpit in a nearby town. While preaching that Sunday morning, he collapsed and died. George wouldn't have wanted it any other way.

I attended his funeral. As expected, the church was packed and because the sanctuary was full, I sat in a room off to one side. I was pleased that his current pastor conducted the service.

Under my breath I said, "George, I'm here, just like I told you I would be."

PLEASE DON'T TAKE
THAT AWAY FROM ME

FOR THIRTY-FIVE YEARS, AS A LOCAL CHURCH pastor, I wrestled with how my congregations would meet their budgets. While our income was far less, our family giving was usually among the top five percent. I never ceased to be amazed at affluent members who gave little or nothing, yet expected to have a strong voice in how everyone else's money should be spent. I finally refused to allow anyone to be nominated to the finance committee whom I knew gave nothing or far below their potential. Those types were rarely interested in what the church could do, but much more concerned with how it could *do without*.

A man may drive an expensive car everyone knows costs over $50,000, live in a house worth several hundred thousand, show off his wall-to-wall plasma TV, eat at expensive restaurants, but become squeamish if asked what he gave to the Community Chest. He brags about holding season tickets to professional or college football games, membership in the country club, a condo in Colorado, but turns red in the face if his preacher suggests he consider tithing. People are funny about money.

Donors come in three types. The first are those faithful ones who promise to give a certain amount and though it might be a strain, fulfill that pledge, and often give beyond what they pledge.

The second are those who promise more than they can achieve and regularly come up short. Some become habitual over-committers and one learns to discount their stated amount when planning the budget. One man I knew annually made the largest pledge in the congregation. Most years he never paid a dime.

The third group falls in the under-achiever category. They have the potential for giving far above what they do. They seem not to consider their giving as an act of faith. Often their annual commitment remained the same year after year, even as their incomes increased. As pastor I learned to love them and worked hard at caring for all, no matter the size of their gifts.

Occasionally, someone discovers joy in stewardship when a project or mission awakens a passionate response. They rise to new levels of financial sharing and personal involvement to discover an odd truth – what is given away does not impoverish, it enriches.

Ministers are not immune to the inadequate giving syndrome. Some say, "Since my income is so low, I more than make up my tithe by the long hours I work for the church." Such a rationale never washes with the laity, and preachers of this persuasion are not highly respected among the membership. Nor do they inspire laity to increase their own donations.

Our family's journey to tithing was inspired by an incident in Hydro, the first church I served after seminary. The community was blessed with a large number of pensioners who lived on small monthly government stipends.

I learned that Miss Effie, in her 80s, was receiving $70 a month on which to live, and out of that she wrote a check for $7.00 to the church. In my youthful ignorance I reasoned that she must believe tithing was an iron-clad law of scripture. Did she fear she would be thought unfaithful, or be un-loved of God, if she did not rigidly follow this ancient custom?

She needed to be relieved of these ideas and be assured that God would love her without such a sacrifice. All who knew Miss Effie were aware of her long years of service to her church. She had earned her stripes – she needn't prove her faith to anyone.

I decided, as her pastor, I was the one to so inform her.

I called and asked to drop by the next afternoon and visit. She was delighted. The aroma of fresh baked goodies wafted about me as she ushered me into her home. The kettle began to sing. Miss Effie scurried into the kitchen and reappeared with cups of steaming hot tea and warm cookies.

She lived in what was called a shotgun house. The front door opened onto the living room which held two occasional chairs and a sofa. A Philco radio rested on a small stand with a reading light and dial phone next to the chair where Miss Effie always sat.

At the other end of the room was the walnut dining table and chairs with matching sideboard. The kitchen was behind that, then the bathroom and finally her small bedroom. Here she had dwelt for several years. When her husband died she had moved out of the big house where they had raised their children and lived for almost fifty years.

Our conversation was lively. While unable to get out much she stayed abreast of the life of the church and asked about several people, commented on our children's program, and inquired about my family. I kept pondering how I might approach the subject of her tithing. She would, I thought, be relieved when I explained that it was unnecessary for her to give at that level. Still, it was not an easy subject to bring up.

Finally, filled with what I thought to be pastoral compassion, I found the courage to tell her why I had come. I said I knew how much of her small stipend she was giving and wanted her to know she didn't have to continue. I pointed out that the tithe, while a fine tradition, was nowhere required by Jesus nor the Old or New Testaments. I spoke of how the germ of it had been a voluntary response of Abraham to God's promise to make his descendants as innumerable as the sands on the sea shore.

When I paused and looked up, Miss Effie was weeping quietly, but in neither joy nor relief. Between sobs she said, *I have done almost every job there was to do in the church. I have taught children, was Sunday School Superintendent, and sang in the choir. I cooked dinners, too many to count. I served for years on the Official Board. Now I can't do any of those things. Only occasionally can I even attend church. About the only thing I can still do is pray and tithe. Preacher, please don't take that away from me!*

I was so sure about my intentions and then in an instant saw how foolish I was. I assured her I didn't wish to take anything away from her, and apologized for not understanding what a precious gift her giving was.

I left humbled by the encounter and wondering when my own giving would bring me such joy.

CONTINUING EDUCATION

I THOUGHT THE CHAPEL SERVICES AT THE SEMInary were stiff, cold, and wordy. Growing up in a congregation with little ritual in its worship, I was unfamiliar with high church liturgy.

Seminary clergy wore robes and colorful stoles that I had never seen outside a Catholic or Episcopal setting. Choirs and ministers *processed* from the back, down the center aisle. Pulpits stood, one on either side of a large table. The front was the *chancel* – one of those pulpits the *lectern*, and the table was the *altar*. Those were strange words.

Back in Perry, Oklahoma, we hadn't talked like that. We used the word *altar* but meant the rail where we knelt and prayed or took communion.

I was uncomfortable in this strange world.

Chapel attendance was assumed, but not required, so it became easy to skip. My friends and I played cards, drank coffee or goofed off. Occasionally, to affirm that chapel was as odd as I thought, I dropped in for a service. It was.

Systematic theology, Church history and bible classes were stimulating, and I acquired an excellent theological education. With one exception, I received good marks, but I graduated with little appreciation of the enduring liturgy of the church.

After seminary, Hydro was more like my home congregation. Worship was simple and uncluttered. But I had not anticipated so many dying that year. That first winter the flu claimed twelve elderly people. Holding a funeral a month does not seem a heavy load, but folks don't die on schedule. Some months there were several deaths in a single week.

Planning a service, comforting a family, talking with funeral directors and music providers, plus writing a message for each service was emotionally draining. With sufficient space between, it is possible to collect one's thoughts, but multiple services back to back made preparation burdensome.

I used The Methodist Book of Worship which contained an Order for the Service of the Burial of the Dead, including prayers scriptures, and other helps. By mid-year I had used this ritual so many times I was weary of its sameness and predictability. The week I conducted three funerals in three days, I was exhausted.

As I stood to begin the last service, I was unsure how to help those mourning. They waited expectantly for me to begin. I looked down on these same faces that had been there yesterday and the day before. I felt the hollowness of the oft repeated ritual, but had no other language to offer.

Truth be told, I was not sold on these ancient words having the power to offset the heavy hand of death. I felt I should be able to find contemporary ways to comfort them.

Once more I intoned, *"Jesus said, "I am the resurrection and the life . . . They that believe in me. . ."*

I glanced at the people and saw their anxiety begin to fade.

I continued, *even though they die, yet shall they live.*

Heads nodded in affirmation.

And they that believe in me shall never die . . .

I thought of the innumerable times those words had been spoken, yet the mourners were leaning into them, hearing each phrase as a great bell pealing hope.

Then I understood. They didn't expect me to explain away death. They weren't waiting for my wisdom to comfort them. That was the gift of the liturgy. Those worn words were a candle flame forcing back the darkness.

My job was to lift up the age-old promise.

They would take it from there.

HENRY

My assignment to Hydro, in a wheat-producing community, made me aware of how little I knew about planting and harvesting. A wheat farmer's work comes down to a span of weeks in which his livelihood teeters between success and failure. If rain falls at the right time and hail doesn't, if strong winds don't flatten the stalks in the field, if the land is dry for cutting and the price per bushel holds – then abundance is bestowed and the cycle repeats. Farming is difficult work attended by intense watching and waiting.

Henry Entz was of German descent and, though he had lived his whole life in Oklahoma, he spoke with a thick accent. He was a stocky, strong man, ruddy complexioned, with hands like ball gloves. He farmed vast sections of land and he cared with a big tender heart.

Once he mentioned that the wheat was in bloom. I asked him what that looked like. He loaded me in his pickup and drove out to the field. Kneeling in the dirt, he lifted a slender stalk and pointed at the barely visible orange bloom called an awn. He told me how the plant develops, why it does or doesn't mature into grain. Then he sifted some loamy soil through his fingers. "Preacher, dat's clean money." Proud of his work, he saw the connectedness of life and knew his occupation was honorable and essential.

Each week, that spring, I drove 285 miles back to the seminary, leaving Paula and two small children at the parsonage. When storm clouds threatened, Henry drove into town, picked up my family, and took them to his home. His wife, Blanche, had readied one of the basement bedrooms. I always knew they were safe.

Henry decided I should have hands-on knowledge of the work of my farming families. He summoned me one fall afternoon, instructing me to come dressed for work. He took me to a field where a huge tractor was waiting. I was about to learn to plow. I had never driven any machine that large, but such decisions were not negotiable with Henry. For several weeks when my daily tasks of caring for a congregation ended, I plowed – late into the night. I discovered my parishioners spent a good deal of time in solitary contemplation. *Plowing wasn't so bad.*

Once all the fields were tilled, Henry called again. Now I was to plant wheat. Back on the tractor, but this time hitched to a drill extending twenty feet behind. On top a long bin held the grain. As the tractor pulled, discs spread open the soil in rows and seed dropped. That was the theory.

This won't be hard.

Driving straight was easy. However, making a U-turn near the end of the field was not. Precise timing was required to wheel the rig around and not hit the fence with the drill, or allow it to back up. If the equipment rolled backward, even the slightest, the tubes jammed into the soil, plugging the holes. Then I had to climb down and cleaned out each tiny cylinder. For a while I performed this correction at each attempted turn around. With practice, however, I soon learned when to turn without a rollback.

The next spring, before harvest, I was relieved to be appointed across state to another church. I didn't want to see how many rows were devoid of wheat where I had sown.

Henry probably smiled at the year's less-than-full crop, but pleased he had taught his preacher about the work and strength of people who till the soil and bring forth a harvest.

TOO MANY COOKS

IN WHEAT COUNTRY EVERYONE LIVES DEEP IN the rhythm of planting and reaping. When harvest begins, farmers are frenzied to bring the crop in before the rain or hail descends. Combines roll from the earliest possible moment to half-past dark. A whole year's labor hangs in the balance.

During harvest that first year in Hydro, I became frustrated trying to get folks to attend the monthly meeting of the Church Board. They were too busy, but in my youthful obedience to what I understood was *the Methodist way*, I persisted. I was the youngest pastor they'd ever had, and no doubt the least aware of their way of life.

Early in the day, the moisture in the wheat can be too high to allow cutting to begin until mid-morning, so I proposed we have a breakfast board meeting. I offered to fix it, which was not an idle boast, as I had cooked for large groups and was confidant. With some grumbling, they agreed.

A couple of the non-farmers, Claude Bixler and Alvin Davis, offered to help me. I'd purchased the food the day before and rose early to begin preparations. Knowing it took a long time for a one hundred-twenty cup percolator to make a full pot of coffee, it was the first thing I started. Java, made in such large quantities, has a tendency to be bitter. But if you lightly salt the grounds as it perks, the harsh taste disappears. This I did.

My two helpers arrived, and we readied a great country breakfast of fluffy scrambled eggs, country ham, crisp bacon, and biscuits with cream gravy. But my assistants figured the seminary curriculum didn't included culinary techniques. Without consulting me, or each other, they assumed I wouldn't know about the pinch of salt. Each quietly lifted the urn lid and added a few shakes. The result, of course, was just short of brine.

The early attenders arrived, sauntered over to the pot, and drew off steaming cups. One sip told them the awful truth. But, thinking their pastor had made the mistake and not wanting to embarrass him, they said nothing. Cups were set aside in a grand conspiracy of silence.

The rest of the meal was a hit, and all ate heartily. After everyone was served, we three cooks sat down to eat and took a sip. We almost gagged. A quick conference revealed that too many cooks can spoil the broth or, in this case, the brew. The whole group had a good laugh.

I still can't remember why I thought we had to have that Board meeting.

YOU CAN GO HOME AGAIN, BUT PROBABLY SHOULDN'T

My life has been an exhilarating journey. I've lived in small villages and metropolitan cities – been a pastor to the dirt poor and some wealthy beyond measure. It has been an honor to be present with people at the birth of their babies, the marrying of their children and the last illnesses and final goodbyes for their loved ones. What a wonder to be allowed into such tender places in people's lives. I am blessed with a loving, devoted wife, Paula, worthier than my shortcomings deserve. My children enrich my life and have blessed me with grandchildren and great grandchildren. I am proud of them and am thankful for so much.

All of this happened from going off to college, seminary and more than a half a century in the ministry. Education opened me to the world. The most enjoyable people I know are those who continue to grow, stretch their minds and remain lifelong students.

I used to joke that I wasn't in the top half of my high school class – but did help make it happen. It was a good line but not really true. Let's say that my grades were medium to well done.

After high school I enrolled at Oklahoma A&M for two reasons. First, it was only twenty-four miles from home and, truth be told, I was not yet ready to go further. Second, it was the college where my brother had attended, and my family roots went back to Stillwater. I wanted to enroll at our Methodist Oklahoma City University, but it seemed too expensive.

If I thought the first year would be a snap, my freshman English teacher, Mrs. Chambers soon dispelled that expectation. Her first assignment was to write a paper on why we had come to college. I set about the task eagerly. When she returned the paper, it was covered with red marks. What a blow to my confidence.

A second discouraging experience centered on the required first semester freshman orientation class. The professor taught with the assumption that no first year college student had a clue about what to do with his or her life and needed his guidance to discover their true path to fame and fortune.

I was clear about my call to ministry and found the professor's exercises tedious. I received a C in the course, with the notation that I had no definable goals and should take his class over. I declined.

The following year, thanks to a scholarship, I was able to leave A&M and attend Oklahoma City University. I planned on a major in history, due to Professor Manikin's excellent American history class in Stillwater. However, at OCU the lectures of the only history professor in that department were certifiably boring.

Dr. Cleveland, the psychology prof, proclaimed on the first day of class, "Where there has been no learning, there has been no teaching." If we attended, did the required reading, and took the tests, we could not flunk. I declared my major in psychology.

Why, if I was going into ministry, didn't I major in religion? I took classes in that department, including Greek and New and Old Testament, but our advisors said seminaries preferred students not do that. When you got to the graduate level you would have to unlearn much of what you'd been taught.

My favorite religion teacher was Dr. Theron C. McGee. He had begun in the Southern Baptist tradition but discovered he did not believe their tenets and found his way to the Methodists. Once, when the subject came up of God speaking to people, he told of a time when he pastored a small Baptist congregation. One Sunday a woman came to tell him that while she was praying that morning, God told her to sing a solo in church. He knew her to be a person of challenged musical abilities and said, "Oh, when did God tell you that?"

"Early, during my devotional time," she said.

Dr. McGee replied, "Well, I just spoke with God a few minutes ago and he said he changed his mind but couldn't reach you because you had left for church."

Just before my senior year at OCU, I was elected vice-president of the Student Senate. I chaired the committee to rewrite the student government by-laws. We worked diligently for most of the school year.

Our efforts required approval by Dr. C.Q. Smith, the University President, who did not think students should have many rights – especially not in print. Before the end of the year we had prevailed and he signed off on our work. It had been years since that had been accomplished by a student senate. I was proud to leave a small legacy.

After seminary we returned to Oklahoma. A year later I was on the OCU campus for a meeting and dropped by the Student Senate Office where I found students busy around a long table.

I introduced myself and told them I had been student vice-president. I asked, "What are you all up to, these days?"

"Oh," replied the young woman chairing the meeting, "we are revising the student by-laws. They haven't been updated for years."

I left quietly.

You can go home again, but probably shouldn't.

THURMAN

A YEAR AFTER SEMINARY, THE REVEREND DR. Andy Coleman invited me to join his staff at University Church in Tulsa. My family and I had grown to love the people in Hydro, but we were ready to move. I took the job and became the Associate Pastor, Director of Christian Education and the Wesley Foundation, our college-student program. Later I realized I had signed on for three full-time jobs.

Dr. Coleman had salt-and-pepper hair, a rugged but handsome face and was of medium stature, the picture of dignity. His eloquent sermons, with illustrations from classic literature, lasted twenty minutes on the dot. An administrative genius, he planned all meetings to insure the desired outcomes. Sensing my over-eager nature, he cautioned me before every board meeting not to speak as he had taken care of everything.

I anticipated an opportunity to preach while he was on vacation. Instead he invited a visiting clergy. I had been there two months and he was unwilling to risk a Sunday service to my unproven skills.

That July, Rev. McFerrin Stowe, pastor at St. Luke's in Oklahoma City, was elected a Bishop. By that fall, the process of filling that opening created a string of moves across our Annual Conference, including my senior minister, Dr. Coleman.

His replacement at University Church was the Reverend. Dr. Thurman Harris, short, balding – ruddy complexioned. He was a contrast to Reverend Coleman's distinguished bearing and pleasant voice. The new pastor's sermons were delivered in staccato bursts. His voice harsh. Illustrations now were from contemporary life – psychology, sociology, current headlines, and quotes from the *United Methodist Social Principles*. Dr. Coleman's sermons had persuaded – Thurman's convicted.

The next twenty-one months were the most exciting and stimulating time of my early career. The rest of my ministry bore the marks of Thurman's influence.

He was a liberal of the first order. Born in New Mexico, he grew up acutely aware of the effects of poverty and prejudice. He believed Jesus' followers were called to be concerned about the down-and-out. He held that the Bible, rightly discerned, impelled Christians to apply its principles to their daily lives. Government was to be on the side of the poor. When it wasn't, a minister of the Gospel should point out those failings and call for reform. This Thurman did with uncommon clarity, and unusual rapidity, it sometimes appearing to lack compassion for the up-and-in folks.

Most in the congregation were middle-class working people, many employed by large oil firms in Tulsa. They were company loyalists, politically conservative, and unaccustomed to their minister attacking big business, corporate greed, and government policy.

This shift in style shocked the congregation and was bound to lead to conflict. Some voiced anger, a few left for churches with less strident preaching. Many others relished his weekly sermons.

From the first, Thurman treated me as an equal and invited me to give the sermon when he was away. He decided we should do a series of Sunday night sermons on current and controversial social issues. He proposed we preach on alternative evenings, with the other leading a question and answer period after the sermon. Sharing these services, fraught with danger to be sure, were heady experiences.

On one of those nights Thurman preached on Fidel Castro's recent overthrow of Cuban dictator, General Batista. America was in a state of alarm about the Communist threat ninety miles off our coast. He thought it important we understand our government's complicity with Batista and how the United States had failed to insist on the establishment of a real democracy in Cuba. His homework was thorough. He claimed the United States allowed poverty to increase among the Cubans, and the dictator to become wealthy, by holding down the price of sugar at the Cuban market, and reaping a great profit when sold in America. Only inferior schools were available to Cuban children while the one school for American kids was of high quality. In short Thurman claimed our government's lack of concern about the poorest of the poor had, in fact, fostered the Communist uprising.

During the discussion that followed I fielded irate statements, wild denials and blind patriotic assertions. I felt as if I was batting bumble bees with a ping-pong paddle. Thurman sat back and, I think, enjoyed my learning experience.

His sharp wit was legendary. The Wesley Foundation students met each week for breakfast and often Thurman joined us at the college cafeteria. On one occasion he ordered a scrambled egg from the less-than-pleasant woman behind the counter. She responded curtly, "We don't scramble just one egg!" As quickly he replied, "Well scramble two. Is it all right if I just eat one?"

Over the next several months tensions in the church didn't subside, nor did Thurman's preaching become less challenging. One Sunday he said, "David and I hear some of you don't like us. Well, that's okay – we don't like some of you." Following the service he ducked out a side door and left me dealing with angry parishioners.

At the end of the second year, I was ready to ask for a church of my own. Unrest in the congregation indicated either Thurman or I should leave. I told the District Superintendent I thought it best be me. He agreed and said doing so would make it possible for Thurman to stay awhile longer. I made an appointment to visit with our bishop.

Bishop Angie Smith greeted me warmly and when I shared my desire to move, congratulated me. "No man worth his salt should be an associate for more than two years."

He concluded with a parting shot at Thurman, who had, on more than one public occasion, been a thorn in his side.

"Thurman likes to shock people. The only trouble is – sometimes he electrocutes them!"

Thurman challenged us to a level of commitment beyond national preferences, political leanings, and anemic Christianity. Clergy who worked with him were enriched by the freshness and intentionality of his life and, in our own ministries, were challenged to speak truth to power.

When he died, his former associates gathered at his funeral and told "Thurman stories" in celebration of his unique life. We laughed and cried at the same time.

I think of Thurman when I imagine a fiery Old Testament prophet.

He was that indeed.

HAM AND WRY

I MUST HAVE BEEN EIGHT WHEN I WAS GIVEN A small part in the school Christmas play. I was cast as a poor man – perhaps a portent of my future. My one line was, "Oh, thank you. Twenty-six cents, just enough to buy bread and cheese and milk for the baby"

We rehearsed for weeks and I never muffed my part. The night of the play my scene appeared. Facing the audience – with my best eight-year-old voice I declared, "Oh, thank you, twenty-six cents, just enough to buy bread and milk and *cheese for the baby*."

Frank Taylor, two years older, red-headed and burley, sat on the front row. When Frank heard *cheese for the baby*, he roared with laughter. Other kids joined in. The audience began to giggle and chortle, enjoying my misread. I, of course, hadn't a clue. I froze a few seconds, and then joined the hilarity. A comedian was born. Laughter was good. It might have gone the other way. I could have panicked and all my life been plagued by stage fright. Since that night I have never feared an audience. Tension in public speakers and performers is healthy, and often I experienced that, but never paralyzing fear.

In time, I became adept at using humor in preaching and teaching. Some dour and sad Christians, especially preachers, deny the joy God intends for us all.

Most of my life I have been something of a ham. Once, when the Cub Scout leader announced we would hold a talent show, I embarrassed my mother by asking, "Can we tell little moron jokes?"

In high school I landed a part in most of the plays. I considered a life on the stage and after my call to ministry even thought of attending seminary in New Jersey because New York City, and Broadway, would be just across the river. In theology school I acted in television plays produced by the drama department at Southern Methodist University. It was good training and because it was the pre-tape era it was essential to be able to ad lib.

For many years I joyfully participated in the gridiron show at our Annual Conference. I loved writing humorous lines and monologues and delivering them for laughs. My friends said I was quicker with a funny line than to quote a scripture. Jesus' harshest words were for those who oppressed the poor or thought themselves more righteous than others. To the rest he spoke gently and with humor.

As a young associate pastor at University UMC in Tulsa, I prepared one Sunday to read the opening lines for the Communion Service. In the older approved text of that day I was to recite from Isaiah

40 ... *Those who wait upon the Lord shall renew their strength; they shall mount up with wings, as eagles.*

In my best ministerial voice, the last of that phrase came out, "*they shall rise up with ings as weagles ...*" I heard me say it, but thought no one else had, so I pressed on with ... *they shall run and not be weary; they shall walk and not faint.*"

But Sanky Birch, a choir member in the loft just above had heard me and stifled a laugh, but his large body shook. His jollity quickly rippled through the basses, tenors, altos and sopranos and out into the congregation. Soon all joined in the laughter and I had to stand there until composure was restored.

If you don't show up in life with humility, it will be supplied ... endlessly.

SACRED SPACE

SACRED SPACE IS PRESENT WHEREVER PEOPLE bestow awe and reverence upon some object or place. It abounds in the midst of a world of pervasive secularism.

Towering cathedrals, stately edifices and white-framed country houses of worship dot our landscape. Across the globe sites are set apart by human devotion.

Even the secular may become hallowed. The Lincoln Memorial, the Tomb of the Unknown Soldier, the Alamo, Oklahoma City's Federal Building, and the World Trade Center in New York City have become consecrated soil. The human species is hard-wired for devotion.

As a child I learned about sacred space in my home church.

One Sunday, Mrs. Fillmore, an elderly lady of the congregation, came down the center aisle headed for her favorite pew and discovered it occupied by visitors. Every Sabbath, for as long as anyone could remember she had sat by herself in that spot.

Room was available in other areas. Surely she would recognize the joy of having visitors, and sit elsewhere. But sacred space trumped radical hospitality. In that pew she did not feel alone but experienced the presence of her long departed husband and now dispersed family.

She stood at the end of the row, staring down at the intruders. She never uttered a word. The visitors moved over to allow Mrs. Fillmore to reclaim her sacred space.

While preparing a memory book of my career, Paula asked what I had learned in the two years I served as an associate pastor. I recalled three things. First, I learned from a pair of wonderful senior pastors, one a classical sermon preacher and the other a prophetic firebrand. Each approach was a gift to me as I formed my own style of preaching.

Second, I encountered for the first time in my young career, an informed layman who knew our *Book of Discipline* better than me. These are the rules by which our church functions. In a meeting an issue arose that I said wasn't covered in the Discipline. Ray Freeman said he thought it was and reached into his briefcase, pulled out a well-marked Discipline, and read the section out loud. I was embarrassed, but had to acknowledge he was right.

Third, I learned a lesson about holy relics.

Years before, this unique congregation had erected a magnificent sanctuary of stone, hewn from a nearby quarry. Most of the construction of the building was done by church members. Artisans from the old country created the stained glass windows that beautified their worship setting. In the center of the chancel a wooden panel rose to the arched ceiling behind an altar table adorned with a large brass cross. The church was a fine reproduction of an English Gothic cathedral. But on this column hung an imposing rendition of Warner Salman's *Head of Christ*. To my recently trained, if less than tried, theological mind that painting seemed out of place. The cross, I reasoned, should not be overshadowed by a mere picture.

The senior minister went on vacation and I was invited to preach. The first Sunday he was away was Communion Sunday. I would, for the first time with this congregation, be the celebrant of the Sacrament of the Lord's Supper.

As the week progressed I became increasingly bothered by that picture. Finally, I made the decision to remove it, just for Communion.

Friday afternoon the custodian helped me put it in a storeroom. The eye now focused on the cross. It was a proper improvement. I congratulated myself.

Saturday afternoon the people preparing the communion elements arrived and set about filling tiny glasses with grape juice and placing communion wafers on small silver trays. This task is usually done by long-tenured members. They see it as a privilege and take pride in the details of the sanctuary. Order and continuity were important, not change.

They were the first to sound the alarm about the missing icon. The general consensus was that it was the work of the associate pastor. I suspect the custodian snitched on me.

Finally, it was agreed to let everything go forward without challenge and we had a fine worship service. People were polite, if reserved, in their comments.

Sacred Space

With experience, pastors learn to read signs of impending doom which, in my youth, I did not yet recognize. One of these is when the congregation's leading lay person hangs back, waiting to speak to you. It rarely means you are about to get good news.

The lay leader told me a meeting had been called of the Trustees and some Board Members for that afternoon to deal with a matter of great importance. They would like me to attend. There was no hint of what was to come. I should have noticed the steely glint in his eyes.

I was pleased. I thought, in the senior pastor's absence, they wanted my advice on some weighty issue. As it turned out, some wanted my head on a platter, and not necessarily a silver one.

The meeting was stormy, and amidst words of "don't you ever again," I was instructed on the limits of my decisional powers, and only spared by the kindness of a few who thought that, in spite of my actions, there might be something in me worth salvaging.

The picture was in its accustomed place before the meeting began.

Ah, sacred space . . . you never know where it will turn up.

BISHOP W. ANGIE SMITH

Bishop W. Angie Smith ordained me a Deacon then an Elder in the Methodist church. He appointed me to my first six churches, and was larger than life.

In 1939, after being separated for almost a century, the Methodist Episcopal Church, the Methodist Episcopal Church South, and the Methodist Protestant Church re-united. They dropped the words Episcopal and Protestant from the titles and formed The Methodist Church. One racial and five geographical Jurisdictions were created within the United States. Oklahoma was in the South Central Jurisdiction. At its first conference in 1944 it elected and assigned W. Angie Smith as Oklahoma's first resident bishop.

Thirty-seven years after statehood, Oklahoma Methodism was small, scattered and disorganized. Bishop Smith was about to change that dramatically.

Soon after arriving in Oklahoma he was asked what he liked. He replied, "I like things big and righteous." In the twenty-four years of his reign, Oklahoma Methodism achieved both. When he retired in 1968, the Oklahoma Conference was among the top ten in the denomination in membership, institutional ministries and evangelism.

After World War II, returning G.I.s who became preachers, were naturals for Bishop Smith to select as District Superintendents. They understood *discipline* and *chain of command*. They possessed the skills to *enforce* the Bishop's vision among the *troops* who were not used to *regimentation*. All learned that bucking the system could land you in the Oklahoma panhandle, or New Mexico, over which he was also the bishop. Un-questioned obedience was a virtue and a career enhancer.

Evangelism was Smith's passion. New member quotas, especially professions of faith, were set for every church. Pastors were required to report net gains and losses. Church membership grew rapidly. Preachers with the most increases were promoted. Others were said to *move on level*.

Unfortunately, the pressure to show net gains in membership caused a few clergy to pad the rolls. Pastors who followed them discovered they couldn't locate everyone listed. In one church I detected that a previous pastor had developed a neat scheme. When Bill Jones and Ann Brown joined, the membership register also reflected a non-existent Ann Jones and Bill Brown. And cleaning the rolls was tantamount to heresy. District Superintendents fought that practice because they too were subject to the *no net loss* rule.

When Bishop Smith arrived most clergy weren't seminary trained. For those who had little education, it was a badge of honor and the claim of an *untainted faith* to not have attended graduate school. An oft-heard statement made by old timers to those of us who did was, "Well, it'll take you about ten years to *ferget* all that stuff." To his credit Bishop Smith encouraged young clergy to seek higher degrees. The Methodist Church insisted that it should have a well-educated clergy.

However, as more trained clergy entered the ranks, they chafed under the highly regimented top-down leadership of Bishop Smith. Attempts to oppose any issue that the Bishop favored at an Annual Conference was quashed by a member of the old guard calling for a standing vote. These always passed, as the Bishop would assign the District Superintendents as counters. If you had the courage to stand and vote the *wrong way*, you knew it would be reported to the bishop.

By the mid-1960s, seminary trained clergy were a rising majority and began to push back at the bishop's sovereign rule. A few of his *druthers* were successfully challenged; an insurance program was defeated and, over his objection the Conference voted to join the State Council of Churches. The Bishop greatly influenced those selected as delegates to the quadrennial meeting, called the General Conference. Gradually some of his choices were replaced by the election of younger, ascending leaders.

Not that he was uncaring of his flock. One preacher standing in line to shake hands, commented, "I don't know why I bother to go through these exercises. He doesn't really know me, or anything about me." About that time he reached the bishop, and as he shook his hand Angie said, "Why Bill, how are you, how are the folks down at First Church? How is your wife Sally? I hear she has been sick. I hope she's better. Are your kids, Tim and Joyce, doing well in college?" Bill walked away stunned.

It was difficult not to be in awe of Bishop Smith, but awe is a second cousin to fear. Because he had so much power over their lives and careers, many people held resentments and hard feelings toward him.

He knew the day of his leadership style was near an end. After he retired he was reported to have said to Bishop Kennedy, "Gerald, there aren't any more giant oaks left – only saplings." He was also heard to say to someone, "There isn't anything more useless than a retired Methodist bishop." He died less than two years after retirement.

The General Conference realized that reassigning bishops to the same conferences over many years could have serious drawbacks. They were elected for life, but the General Conference finally placed a twelve-year limit in any one Annual Conference. Some said, primarily because of Angie and one or two other autocrats, *no one will ever again serve that long in one place.*

His accomplishments were monumental. But twenty-four years in power is a long time. Had he retired earlier, there may have been fewer bad memories.

For me, it was a journey which began in my youth with awe, turned to fear, then anger and now, after long years of reflection, respect.

There will never be another Angie Smith. Perhaps one was enough.

SHORT, SHORT STORIES

Didn't See that Coming

THE REV. MOUZON ROSSER WAS KNOWN FOR his inability to stay more than two years at most churches before the congregation requested he be moved. In those days preachers didn't find out where they were moving until the Bishop publicly read their assignments the last day of Conference.

Once, Mouzon came to Conference in an unusually happy frame of mind. Everyone expected he was moving and wondered why he was so cheerful.

Mouzon said, "I've looked through the Journal at all the places they could send me, and none are as bad as where I am."

He listened while the bishop intoned the names of churches followed by the name of the assigned preacher. When Mouzon's was announced he was heard to remark, "Damn, I forgot about that one!"

A Man Can Hope, Can't He?

Mouzon Rosser was a big man, over six feet tall and more than 300 pounds. He was gifted with a wry sense of humor. And when he laughed he snorted through a rosy bulbous nose.

We served together in the Ardmore District in southern Oklahoma. I was a student and would begin my seminary training that fall.

In August the District Superintendent called a meeting of all clergy and encouraged everyone to share a word about their church activities over the summer. This became an occasion for can-you-top-this brags. Attendance numbers were suspected of being inflated, as were accounts of professions of faith and financial solvency.

Mouzon was the last to speak. He rose from the back pew, scratching his head as if trying to think. Then with a laugh, punctuated by snorts, he said, "We'll, we've had two funerals this summer, and "(*snort, snort*), hoping for a third!"

We Got You Covered

Mouzon was on a trip with two preacher buddies. They stopped for lunch and he told the friends he didn't have much money with him. The friends finished their meal and said they'd take care of his bill as they went out, and they'd meet him at the car.

They said, "When we get to the cash register, wave so the man will know who we are covering."

At the front they said, "That guy back there has the check and will take care of our tab." They pointed to Mouzon, who waved. When Mouzon started to leave without paying, the manager followed him outside and accused him of stiffing the waitress. The man was on the verge of calling the cops, when the two friends came to his rescue.

Lord, Save Me from My Friends

My friend Mac Thompson told of being summoned to Bishop Smith's office. Mac had no clue why he was there.

The Bishop said, "Mac, someone told me you recently said some rather unkind things about me. Is that true?"

Mac thought for a moment. "Bishop, I have two comments. First, I said it. And second, I thought I was among friends *when* I said it."

Mac reported that the Bishop laughed and for twenty minutes, recounted how he had experienced similar betrayals from so-called friends.

Empty Nesters

While serving at Mayfair UMC in Oklahoma City, I had a Sunday school class of adults whose young-adult children were leaving home for colleges or careers. The parents' separation anxiety was palpable.

I thought Mac Thompson was the person to speak to these parents about the *empty nest syndrome*. I called him and explained my need. Would he come?

Mac paused. "Well, I guess I can, but I have to tell you – mine keep flying back to the nest."

No Time for Prayer

Attending my first Annual Conference session in 1951, I listened to the hotly debated proposal to merge the West Oklahoma and the East Oklahoma Annual Conferences. Clearly Bishop Smith was for the union as were most of those present. For several years it had been under consideration and, a year before, the East Conference had voted in favor. It remained for the West to confirm and form The Oklahoma Annual Conference.

Among those who seemed opposed to consolidation was the Reverend Charles Wells, who was, at the time, one of the younger members of the conference. Just as the bishop was about to put the question to a vote, Charles rose to object. Perhaps hoping that appealing to the Almighty might *drag the conference over to his position,* he said, "Bishop Smith, I think before we take this action we should take time to pray about it."

Bishop Smith looked down from his elevated chair, fixing Charles for a moment with *that look,* and said, "Young man, you've had a year to pray about this. It's time to vote."

I thought, my, my, a bishop who doesn't want to pray.

It All Depends

At a time when it was considered unwise to openly challenge the wishes of Bishop Angie Smith, there was one who did so regularly. The Reverend Doctor

Thurman Harris loved to debate, especially if it provided an opportunity to oppose something the bishop favored.

On one occasion, Thurman had left the conference floor. An issue arose over which there was clearly a divided house. Thurman returned just before the vote and someone asked him, "How are you going to go on this?"

Thurman replied, "Hell, I don't know – which side is Angie on?"

My Cigars, Please

In 1939 the union of the three divided Methodist bodies took place. They had been separated for almost a century. In the negotiations leading up to the merger there were major issues – and some not so major, but important to one or the other uniting groups. Among the not-so-important were differences over the use of alcohol and tobacco. The Methodist Episcopal Church, the so-called northern church, seemed less concerned about the temperate use of alcohol but forbade its clergy to smoke, while The Methodist Episcopal Church, South, or southern church, was strongly anti-alcohol, but thought smoking a lesser sin. Each group agreed to give up their preference for a new church stance squarely against both.

Bishop Angie Smith was a southerner, and he loved his cigars, but gave them up, at least in public. However, some of the missionaries of the old southern church had been out of the country for many years and upon returning either didn't remember or didn't care about the ban. One of them, visiting from Cuba, presented Bishop Smith with a box of the famous Cuban cigars during an Annual Conference session. The bishop stammered, "Well, well, I can't accept it, but you might give it to Brother Dewey Etchison, the Superintendent of the Oklahoma Indian Mission. I think he may still use them."

Few knew, but the bishop and Etchison had adjoining cabins on Lake Texoma in southern Oklahoma. It was told that when they met there, soon after conference, the bishop said, "Dewey, give me my cigars!"

Our Preacher Can't Sing

Bishop Smith told of a visit once by a group of lay people from a small Oklahoma church. They told him that they wanted their preacher moved. He inquired as to why – was he a bad preacher?

"No, they said, his sermons are okay, but he can't sing."

Bishop Smith replied, "Well, I didn't send him there to sing."

They replied, "You don't understand, Bishop, he doesn't know he can't sing."

Depends on which Way He was Running?

While we were out west in Buffalo, the local Roman Catholic Priest, Father Paul Gallatin and I became good friends. We discovered we had much in common, especially in a community dominated by fundamentalist preachers.

He had spent most of his life in boarding school, seminary and in a congregation in Oklahoma City, where fine restaurants were available. Moving to Buffalo he discovered a paucity of good eating establishments and had prevailed on Chef John Bennett, at the famous Cellar Restaurant in OKC to teach him to cook. Of course, that was gourmet food. I visited Paul one day at his rectory, and he was in the kitchen.

"What are you cooking, Paul?"

"Chicken Kiev – for one."

On another occasion I found him sitting on the living room floor surrounded by a stack of books. I asked what he was doing.

He said, "Legend says that when DeSoto came through the Panhandle, a priest dropped from the troop to minister to the Native Americans. He was supposedly martyred – and I'm trying to find out if the arrows were in his chest, or his back."

MAY I HAVE A VOLUNTEER, PLEASE

NO PARISH CHURCH FUNCTIONS WITHOUT volunteers. Preachers believe the old adage true, "If you want something done, ask a busy person to do it." Active people do not prolong meetings, hassle over decisions, or assemble unnecessarily. They cut to the chase, find the bottom line and adjourn. Unpaid workers are priceless.

There are, however, two groups who, I believe, receive secret training. These must have attended a *clundestine* school calculated to drive a minister out of his gourd. I speak of *church ushers* (CUs) and *sound system operators* (SSOs). These two essential roles, well done, are delightful – almost invisible but, if done poorly, create chaos.

Ushers (CUs) are the first to greet members and visitors. They seat people and hand out bulletins. They make an accurate count of attendance, take up the offering, keep an eye on the temperature, and are first responders if someone becomes ill, or needs directions to the restroom. These are important tasks that help the worship service run smoothly.

In most congregations the CUs perform with grace and efficiency. But in other churches ushers give less acceptable performances. It may be too strong to dub them "Ushers from Hell," but one wonders whose side they are on.

Take smiling. It should go without saying that CUs need to offer a smile as they seat, hand a bulletin, or pass the plate. But some come from the *school of frown*. I am a regular pew sitter since my retirement, and have said to an usher, "I won't take that bulletin until you smile at me." They rarely forget again.

In some churches ushering is a lifetime appointment. Senior status ushers are reluctant to recruit younger folks to take their place. I'm not suggesting they're too old, but it's rumored some ushered at the Last Supper. Replacing an aging *doorkeeper in the house of the Lord* is a task attempted by only the bravest pastor.

Ushering for communion is a vital task, especially where members come to the front and kneel to receive the elements. You need twenty-two people at the rail, eleven on each side, and that number never changes. For reasons known only to the *guild of ushers*, this appears to be a task beyond their comprehension. At some point an usher steps in front of the twelfth person, leaving the altar half full. The pastor may beg with his eyes – staring at the back of the usher's head to allow more to kneel. However, this usher will compensate at the final table, when he will try to shoehorn in the last thirty people. It is useless to mention this after the service.

Counting attendance provides the pastor with important information. To do this accurately a CU should walk to the front and count everyone as he moves to the back. Again, I think the *Usher Union's* solemn code forbids this and instructs them to count from the back, on tiptoe if necessary, craning their necks. This rule only applies to men. Women do it correctly, but too few are asked to serve in this capacity.

Sound System Operators (SSOs) are the volunteers most skilled at giving the pastor ulcers and running fits. I have long suspected a secret manual exists for SSOs and recently, while digging around in a sound booth for a microphone the SSO has hidden, I discovered such a document. I share it here for the benefit of my colleagues in ministry who have ever wanted to *off* an audio operator, and tell God he died.

Ten Rules for Successful Sound Technicians

1. Never make eye contact with the minister during worship. Clergy are unskilled in technical matters and will only mess up your equipment trying to get you to tweak it. They are best ignored.
2. Do not turn up a microphone until a person has begun to speak or sing. Suddenly increasing the volume will waken sleepy parishioners so they may pay attention. Ministers fail to see how helpful this is and have been known to attempt mayhem on SSOs after church.

3. When playing a tape for a soloist or the choir, develop the skill of leaving about half a minute of dead air before the music begins. This provides time for the congregation to settle down and focus. It also gives musicians ulcers, but no matter, they tend to be high strung anyway.
4. As you become experienced you will sense when the pastor is delivering an unusually great sermon. You know he or she will expect a good recording of it. On these occasions, forgetting to turn on the recorder or *accidently* turning it off in mid-sermon is a true art, especially when performed with an air of innocence. Whimpering clergy are a pitiful sight.
5. Modern sound systems are a marvel. They have bunches of buttons, gadgets and switches. While the minister is preaching provides an excellent opportunity to learn what all those buttons and slides are capable of doing. With practice, you can make the preacher sound like Porky Pig or Darth Vader. You may break Rule #1 on these occasions and look the preacher in the eye, shrug your shoulders as if to say, "I can't imagine what caused that."
6. Microphone placement is important. Putting a mike near the one person in the choir who sings loudest or most off-key adds variety to the worship. Choir directors seem not to appreciate this, but they are so temperamental.

7. Timing is everything. A veteran SSO never enters the sound booth until seconds before the service begins, or perhaps after a few bars of the prelude are played. While little appreciated by the clergy, it is truly a benefit. Good performers require a nervous edge. Also, SSOs should exit the church as quickly as possible after the benediction. No need to speak with the pastor when he is tired and cranky. He will cool down by next week.
8. SSOs must assist the pastor in being ready for the service. If you put his lapel mike on him *live* before he goes to the bathroom, he may enter the sanctuary having already reminded the congregation of their baptism. Symbolic acts are important.
9. SSOs are responsible for the electronic equipment, so locate an impossible-to-find place to secure microphones. Tell no one of this location, especially the minister. The fact that the microphones cannot be located for a mid-week funeral is the price paid to protect expensive property.
10. If the SSO is going to be unavailable for the Sunday service, or has run out of microphone batteries, or recording tapes – never bother the pastor during the week. Call him on Saturday night, around 11 o'clock.

With these few rules diligently followed, a gifted SSO can bring the most confident preacher to his knees, turn choir directors into jibbering idiots and keep a sedate congregation on the edge of their pews wondering what will happen next.

So, here's to volunteers. We don't know how to exist with them and can't live without them.

EXCUSES – LAME, BUT STILL EXCUSES

AFTER TWO YEARS IN TULSA WE REQUESTED a move to the western side of the state because our son, Art, was having so much trouble with asthma. We anticipated the drier climate might help. Prior to moving we visited with Charlie and Donnie Ratliff a lay couple from Hollis, and asked them about trees in that part of the state. Charlie said, "Oh, we have a huge tree in our yard. You can see it for miles." We were headed from green country to the desert southwest part of Oklahoma.

The Hollis United Methodist Men's Club met Wednesday evenings at the church. Twenty or so men, some church members, some not, gathered each week at 6:00 p.m.

Dinners were prepared by rotating teams, the only required ingredient being some form of grease. The preacher was allowed a brief time for a devotional. The rest of the evening was for dominoes which, in this community, was considered a quasi-religious activity.

They were serious players and, when a few younger men put up a ping-pong table in one corner, there was open rebellion. And woe to the preacher who talked more than fifteen minutes – feet began to shuffle, coughs erupted – a signal the preacher was through, even if he wasn't.

Around Christmas and Valentine's Day, they held banquets and invited their wives. At these events the food was less greasy – might even include a green vegetable, and white paper covered the tables. For such occasions the president of the group would turn to me and say, "Preacher, please get up a little program for the ladies." It went without saying that the presentation should be brief, so they could take the wives home and come back to play dominoes. Finding entertaining and short material had become increasingly difficult.

However, on one occasion I had an inspiration. Borrowing a device that could tape phone conversations, I began to call the men of the club. For some, the only religious service they experienced was my Wednesday devotional. Others were used to teaching a Sunday School class or assisting in worship services.

If I thought they wouldn't mind giving a prayer I asked, "Would you explain what the Men's Club is, and what it does?"

I asked Emory Crow, a distinguished banker in the community, to explain. After a long pause he said, "Well, preacher what the hell *do* we do but eat, belch, and get up and play dominoes?"

If I thought they might shy away from public prayer I asked, "Would you give the invocation?" I

Excuses – Lame, but Still Excuses

guessed correctly that many would not even know what that meant.

I asked Pete, the crusty old sheriff, "Would you mind giving the invocation?"

"The *what*?" he sputtered. Had I asked him to wade into a den of thieves he wouldn't have blinked.

I recorded his stammering excuse about how *his voice might not be up to it as he was coming down with a cold*.

As I played back these recordings after the banquet and, as they heard their excuses unfold, they looked sheepishly at their wives. It was a laughter-filled evening and, I am told, long remembered after I moved away.

But Art's asthma doctor in Tulsa had cautioned us that in all likelihood he would develop allergies wherever we lived. He was right. After two years in Hollis, with its annual cotton harvest and accompanying pervasive lint, we requested to change again.

HEARTLAND HEARTBEAT

A half-century ago I came first to this land.
And saw it as barren, inhospitable
lacking in character.

I missed the finer points that commend it.
Now I see it as fertile, receptive
of infinite integrity.

I only anticipated where my future lay.
Focused on the city, erratic, fast paced
challenging my gifts.

I didn't feel the rhythm to which the people pulsed,
The primordial heartbeat, steady, mad-
    deningly slow
yet sanity's keeper.

They were satisfied with sameness, willfully
    unchanging.
Trusting frayed things, tradition, shared innocence
their unalterable fate.

Now I feel their common wisdom, live by
    seasons, not events.
Knowing in the marrow of their bones
peace, hope, serenity.

PRIDE OF PLACE

WE WERE ASSIGNED TO BUFFALO, A FAR northern town at the edge of the Oklahoma Panhandle. It was a move from Hollis, four miles from the Texas line, to six miles from Kansas.

When preachers change locations, they usually rent a U-Haul. For most of our moves we'd been fortunate to pack our belongings in Paula's Dad's pickup. He was a master at piling our stuff high. And we never lost nor had a broken item.

Now, her dad was retired and had sold his pickup. I rented a U-Haul in OKC, drove it to Hollis, loaded our goods and we headed to Buffalo. We unloaded into the house through the front door, and our predecessor, Dean Miller, transferred his goods out of the garage into the same truck and drove it to his new assignment in Oklahoma City. We split the bill.

In Buffalo, a group of parishioners were on hand to welcome and help us get settled into our new home. They brought our first meal. This parsonage, unlike most we had lived in, was not next door to the church, but on the far northwest edge of town.

We were pleased to discover a newly finished sanctuary but not happy to learn that it wasn't paid for. They had previously built a basement and used it for worship. A few years before we arrived they had erected the above-ground classrooms and worship center. They owed about $40,000 on the expansion, a fairly hefty amount in that era.

Studying the financial books, I discovered the outstanding debt had not changed over several years, with only the interest being paid annually. I stewed over this and wondered why.

The Lay Leader of the congregation was Lee Adams, a Farm Bureau agent. One day he and I were riding in his pickup on some errand. I was whining about the un-reduced debt. Without warning, Lee slammed on the brakes and stopped dead in the middle of a gravel farm road. Dust swirled around us, covering the windshield.

He turned to me, "Preacher, let me tell you something about how we live in these parts. We survive from crop to crop. We depend on credit, graciously extended by the bankers of this community. We haven't had a bountiful yield in several seasons. Sometimes we don't make enough to cover the cost of the seed we planted in the fall. One of these years we will have a great harvest, fifty-sixty bushel an acre. When that happens, we'll pay off that note and it ain't gonna do you any good to keep harping on that $40,000. Until then we will take care of the interest only. Understand how we live and you and the congregation will be a lot happier."

Learning how people live should be a seminary course, equal in value to systematic theology. We moved at the end of our fourth year, and soon after they had a bumper crop and paid off the debt. We heard they burned the mortgage with great celebration.

In small communities you also learn that almost everyone is related through birth or marriage. I visited a farm family one day and the conversation turned to strange sights, noted by the lady of the house. I added my thoughts by telling about having seen something in the little town of Ft. Supply, a few miles south of Buffalo.

There was a filling station at the edge of town at the junction where the highway turned north toward Buffalo. It was run by a big man who must have weighed over three hundred pounds. In the hot summer he wore no shirt and his huge belly flopped and sagged in a most disgusting way.

As I related this, I noticed the lady of the house's head drop and her eyes fix on the floor. When I finished she looked up and said, "I know, I know, Dad is an embarrassment to the whole family, but he just laughs when we tell him to put on his shirt."

And when a car passes you going the other way, it's country courtesy, without taking your hand from the steering wheel, to slightly wave a couple of fingers in greeting, even if you haven't a clue who it is. Failing to do that may get you a comment something like, "Hey, preacher, you high-hatted me the other day when we passed on the highway."

There was only one café in town where folks sat down for a meal. I heard that the owner/cook was ill and stopped by and asked if I could do anything to help.

"Can you cook?" they asked.

"Well, yes, some." That *some* referred to my brief stint at the Carter County Free Fair, but I was game, if a bit over-confident. So, for a couple of days, I did short-order cooking at the café. I'm convinced the staff contacted the sick owner and said, "Get back here quick!"

But my volunteering to help out at the newspaper office led to something I hadn't expected. The owner's wife, and editor of the paper, became ill and required surgery. I dropped by to see if I could help Ed, the publisher.

"Can you write stories and sell ads?" Ed asked.

I said I didn't have any experience but was willing to try. So, while his wife recuperated I wrote the stories and visited businesses to secure ads.

Folks who live far from the big cities are proud of their lifestyle and cannot comprehend that you, or anyone, might want to live anywhere else.

Toward the end of that stint I was approached by two businessmen who asked if I would consider a deal regarding the paper. The owner, Ed, was in his eighties, they noted, and he couldn't last much longer. They proposed to form a coalition and buy the newspaper if I would stay and run it.

It was a flattering offer, but it wasn't for me. I was flying by the seat of my pants and had no skills for such a thing. I declined the offer and, had I stopped there, everything might have ended well.

I told them I couldn't do it because I had a calling to be a minister and would soon be moving on. Shutting up even *then* would have been acceptable.

"Besides," I added, "I would like to live in or near Oklahoma City."

Big mistake. One of them said, "You mean you would rather go live in the big smelly city than out here where the air is fresh?"

End of conversation. I was a lost soul, beyond redemption, a man to be pitied, and unworthy of their offer.

They walked away in disgust.

Pride of place is not to be mocked.

COOKIE

WE MOVED TO DRUMRIGHT TO DISCOVER the church was less than a block from Main Street. The parsonage, next door to the church, was about half the size of the home we had left in Buffalo, and with two growing middle school kids, it was cramped. The house was the same English Gothic architecture as the church, including a stained-glass window in the front door. Closets were few and small. Bedrooms were tiny. There was one bathroom. On Sunday the men's bible class met in the living room, and Paula taught youth in the kitchen.

Parsonages, as church-owned living spaces for clergy, may be passing from the scene. Today clergy prefer to own their homes. Over forty-six years we lived in fourteen houses owned by either a local church or our state organization, the Oklahoma Annual Conference. With a few exceptions, we have less than pleasant memories.

Our first parsonage, back in Springer, was two discarded officer's quarters from a nearby defunct Air Force base, scotched together, and put up on blocks – with no skirting. Single deck flooring, with gaps between boards, allowed free passage of mosquitoes, scorpions, and other creepy-crawlies. But the *piece-de-resistance* was the poured concrete bathtub. Nothing like taking a bath and having one's backside defoliated at the same time.

Early on parsonages came furnished except for a few items clergy carried from place to place. Furniture, no longer desired by church members in their own dwellings, often became gifts "for the reverend." This usually resulted in a mismatch of style and colors that Paula and I dubbed *Early American Parsonage*.

Congregations considered their pastor on duty twenty-four-seven so it was logical to have the parsonage next to the church, where he could *look after things*. That included all the panhandlers who stopped by, as well as opening and closing the building for every group that met there during the week. The church being so close, the men's Sunday School class met in our living room. They didn't bother to knock.

Building repairs, or the acquisition of new furnishings and appliances, were in the hands of nine trustees. Often these were older men more intent on saving money than caring about the preacher's comfort.

While an associate pastor in Tulsa, our son had become severely asthmatic. The only relief from the heat was a window water cooler which increased humidity and the growth of mold, making him sicker. The trustees had discussed purchasing a refrigerated air conditioner at the beginning of the next fiscal year, two months away. After Artie was hospitalized

Cookie

because of his asthma, I asked if they would install it early. They refused, saying it wasn't budgeted, even though I knew they had ample reserves. But this insensitivity was not true of all our congregations. In other towns people were more caring.

In Drumright the church folks were wonderful. We were included in community activities and became friends with people outside our congregation. Paula was hired to teach fifth grade, and our kids developed new school friendships.

Each morning at ten and again around four, people gathered at Huff's drugstore for coffee. During these times I could greet most of the business members from our church.

Among the men who frequented the drugstore was Melvin "Cookie" Cook. On Sunday mornings Cookie was our head usher. Sometimes, if he thought I was preaching too long, he'd get up, walk to the back and act out winding the clock on the back wall. I got the message.

In the back room of his insurance agency he had a pool table, and invited me to play pool in the afternoons. Growing up, I'd been forbidden to frequent pool halls where, according to my Mother, *unsavory types gathered*. I was a terrible player. But Cookie and the others were patient and instructive, and in time I occasionally won. It was a time of rich fellowship and good humor, and I was treated not as the preacher but as a regular person.

Other than ushering, I don't recall that Cookie held any office in the church. He was happy for others to attend meetings and make decisions. But that changed in our second year. A few folks began to see how cramped the parsonage was, and thought a new house should be considered. Others saw no reason to change. Then a house came up for sale in a newer section of the community. The seller was offering it for the $10,000 equity he had in it, the new owner to take over the payments.

Cookie was enthusiastic. He offered to help raise the money, and began calling on those he thought could give. Mr. Shanks, a rival insurance agent, was not in favor of the new house. Cookie was persistent.

Finally, Shanks said, "I don't think you can do it, but if you raise $9,000, I'll give the last $1,000."

Later Cookie told me, "I knew I was going to raise that money, just to make him pay up." Indeed, the day they reached the goal, he went straight to Shanks and said, "Get out your checkbook." He did!

We moved into a lovely, spacious, and comfortable home, many blocks from the church. Our new neighbors were among the leading citizens of Drumright. Our children's friends were within walking distance.

I will always appreciate the extra effort from Cookie, to enable a near miracle and provide a new home for the minister and family.

It was the finest dwelling the Severe family had ever occupied.

KANSAS CITY BABE

THE PHONE RANG IN MY STUDY. THE CALLER was a local Drumright funeral director.

"David," he said, "I need a favor."

"Sure Carl. What can I do for you?"

"Kansas City Babe has died and I need someone to do her funeral."

"Who in the world is Kansas City Babe?"

He laughed quietly and said, "Well, at least I am comforted you didn't know her.

During the roaring oil boom days of the 20s and 30s, she ran the most popular brothel in Creek County. After the oil boom ended, and long after prostitution ceased being an openly plied profession, she continued to live in the old multi-storied house, just off Main Street."

She had, Carl explained, frozen to death in the old house. The gas company had cut off the service when bills went overdue for months and demands for payment unanswered.

"I don't think she has any family, and I am willing to cover the expense of a decent funeral, but I need someone to say a few words. I can't stand it that anybody would die and not receive a proper burial. Will you help me out?"

Carl knew most preachers in town wouldn't touch such a service, yet sensed I might. I said I'd do it but wondered what I could say. I knew nothing about this woman, except what I had just been told. Carl didn't think anyone would attend.

The service was arranged for two days later. On a foggy, wintry day I went to the funeral parlor. Carl and I visited in his office for a while and, at the time for the service, I entered the chapel.

Carl had provided a simple coffin, which stood center-front, a small flower display on top.

However, the room was not empty as we had expected. One old man sat near the back. I strained to see his face in the dim light.

As my eyes adjusted, I discovered he was the closest thing to a walking human wreck one might imagine. The miles on his frame may have been more than his years on a calendar. The broken blood vessels of his cheeks and temples told me he'd had a long and personal relationship with alcohol. The skin below his eye sockets drooped, in bloodhound fashion. What had once been the whites of his eyes were now spidery red squiggles and the sunken center dots smoldering black. Moisture from watery eyes had permanently stained his cheeks.

Still, there were traces of grace and shadows of an earlier vigor. In a past time, he had been a handsome man. Unfortunately, his day had long since been flushed away.

I nodded in his direction. No response. He stared at the floor. My brief service was crumbling. I had planned no eulogy, but with someone there I must do something. I decided to read more from the funeral service manual, including additional prayers and scriptures.

I began, "Remember the words of Jesus 'I am the resurrection and the life – he that believes in me. . . "

A strange sound came from the back. He was crying, his chest rising and falling with deep-wrought sobs. He held a tattered bandanna but made no attempt to wipe his eyes. He caught the tears in it as they fell, as if to save them and the memories they evoked.

I read a scripture, then a prayer for comfort. The weeping continued – each tear lamenting a never-to-be-forgotten moment. The ritual was almost over, and my mind raced ahead. I wanted to meet this man who mourned with such anguish. What a story he must have. I hoped he would share it.

Bowing my head for the closing prayer and benediction, I barely noticed the old man slipping out the door. By the time I made my way outside he was gone. He'd vanished in the fog.

Returning to the chapel I sat down where he had been. The unwashed smell of his humanity hovered around me. I looked at the small casket holding the earthly remains of Kansas City Babe. I pondered on what kind of relationship they had shared – surely greater than her profession implied. There was a connection of long standing, a union of spirit, a touch of human frailty wrapped in years of mutual caring. Whatever, Kansas City Babe was taking it to the grave. It was a lead pipe cinch the old man wasn't going to tell. Before long, he would join her in whatever afterlife was granted them.

Over the years, when I've thought about Kansas City Babe and her one mourning friend, I smile and acknowledge the gift of life's mysteries. Some things are not meant to be explained.

THE BODY SWAPPERS

As sad as such occasions are, funny things can happen around funerals. Directors are on call 24/7 like doctors once were. Strong emotional ties bind families to a caring undertaker and they always request that establishment when a family death occurs. Taking time off is not easy.

My undertaker friend, Carl, and his two college-age sons found an opening, with no pending funerals, and decided to go to Colorado for a few days of skiing. Unfortunately, they had barely arrived when Carl came down with the flu. Then the call came from home – *two deaths – return immediately*. The boys bedded Dad down in the back seat – drove all night and deposited him in his bed, assuring him they had helped him in countless funerals and could manage the two services.

The first was scheduled for 10:00 that morning, and the second at 2:00 p.m. They loaded up the first casket and headed for the church.

At the funeral home, out-of-town relatives arrived to pay respects to Uncle Charlie who was to be buried later that afternoon. The attendant ushered them into the viewing room and closed the curtain. Soon she heard voices from behind the drapes.

"Goodness, he doesn't look like himself."

"He must have been very sick."

"Hard to believe that's Uncle Charlie."

They emerged from the room and headed to the family home to share their sadness with their kinfolk.

By now the attendant had figured out what was wrong. The two bodies had been switched. She called the church where the first funeral was to take place and told the sons they had the wrong casket and to get the right one there pronto.

The boys reloaded the real Uncle Charlie and raced to the funeral home, made the switch, and returned in time for the service.

At the funeral home all was well until a family delegation arrived to check why the out-of-towners thought Charlie looked so poorly. Solemnly the attendant escorted them into the viewing room. The voices wafting into the hall were assurances that he looked just fine.

However, when they opened the casket to view the body at the end of that last funeral, the out-of-towners were visibly shaken at how much Uncle Charlie's looks had improved since they last saw him.

When my friend Carl got well and was told what had happened, he nearly had a relapse.

LEARNING INDIAN TIME

THE INVITATION TO PREACH WAS FOR FOUR IN the afternoon. I drove to Bristow from Drumright and at 3:30 pulled into the empty parking lot. The church was dark, the door locked.

My elders in ministry had taught me about *white time. Be prompt – arrive early – never be late. Meetings should start and end on time!*

At 3:45, I reviewed my notes, practiced reading the scripture aloud. *Did I have the right day?* I looked in my date book – this Sunday, Mutteloke Indian Methodist Church in Bristow.

It was a congregation of mostly Euche Native Americans whose history recorded De Soto encountering their ancestors in the 1500s.

They were thought to be descendants of the *Mississippian Mound Builder Culture*. Prior to the US Government's forced removal, the Euches lived in Florida, Georgia and Alabama.

In 1829, Andrew Jackson was elected President and vowed to expel all Indians from the southeastern states. The Euches had been a large tribe but, before 1830, some escaped and joined the Seminoles in Florida. Another group became angry over what they considered the improper performances of the sacred dances. They fled to the far northwest and disappeared into western tribes.

In the early 1830s, fewer than 2000 were brought to Oklahoma and resettled around Sapulpa, Kellyville and Bristow on tribal land known as Duck Creek, Polecat Creek and Sand Creek. When the government refused to acknowledge them as a tribe, they affiliated with the Muscogee Confederacy, but kept to themselves. They feared being absorbed by yet another group. Today they are few in number and strive to keep alive their customs, language, music and tribal dances.

The announced hour for worship passed – no congregation, no pastor. At 4:10 a man emerged a block away and strolled in my direction. He crossed the lawn and disappeared behind the church. Lights came on inside the building. I rattled the door. He opened it.

I said, "Excuse me, sir, is there a worship service here this afternoon?"

"Yep, there is."

"I was told it was at four o'clock. Was that wrong?"

"No, that'd be 'bout right."

"Where are the people?"

"They'll be along. Have a seat."

With that, he left me and went into the back of the building.

I was about to learn about *Indian time*.

The late Rev. David Adair, a Cherokee pastor in the Oklahoma Indian Mission Conference, once told me, "You white folks say we Indians don't start meetings on time. We do. We start when everyone gets here. And we quit on time – when we're done."

The sanctuary seating was wooden benches with slatted backs. The room might have held thirty or forty people. A small table served as the altar. On it sat an open Bible next to a small cross.

At 4:25 a pickup pulled in, followed by several more vehicles. A man I took to be one of the leading lay members welcomed me. Others spoke and shook my hand.

Singing started about ten minutes before five. Hymns were sung in the Euche, Creek, Cherokee, and Choctaw languages. There was no song leader, someone in the group called out a person to begin a hymn, and others joined in. The music continued until the pastor arrived, having driven from Ada where he had visited a member in the Indian hospital. Worship would now begin.

There were no bulletins, but the order was familiar to them all. The pastoral prayer time was heartfelt, but unfamiliar to me. He began and others, moved by the spirit, voiced their own petitions in English or their native language, or in an ecstatic tongue – all speaking at the same time. The pastor continued – his voice rising above the supplications, not finishing until all other voices fell silent. The cacophony made it difficult to understand, but I caught that the prayers were for restoration of health, a wayward family member, and expressions of thanks.

Graciously they received my sermon. But after hearing their prayers, I felt my words failed to touch their collective concerns and pains. I couldn't know the daily struggles they encountered, the victories or defeats they experienced.

My sermon wasn't over their heads, but it may have missed their hearts.

THE WEDDING

I DON'T KNOW HOW THEY MET BUT I'LL WAGER it was a short courtship. Each knew the other was the object of a search that had occupied their days and dreams. Other options seemed unthinkable.

Jeans, boots and western shirts were Mr. Smith's comfort, but he appeared for the ceremony in crisp khakis that reflected his military service. He was not unkempt and was as presentable as he needed to be for the occasion. Being there at all was a miracle. His Sergeant hadn't agreed to grant him leave until the bride-to-be sent him a personal invitation indicating the date, and noting that the groom's presence was required.

Miss Radabaugh, knew something of propriety. She was eager to wear the traditional white gown and veil she had seen in brides' magazines. In her innocence, she may not have understood all that went into such an event. She arrived with her dress and veil crushed into the cardboard box it had come in from the store. But a few quick shakes, and with some assistance from her mother and my wife, and she was ready. The veil, more difficult to tame than the dress, stood at defiant angles, but it perched on her head as regal as a prom queen's tiara.

The bridal march began. The groom, in the usual trance, and best man followed me into the sanctuary. The groom hit the mark where he had been told to stand at rehearsal, turned and gazed in the direction from whence his bride would enter.

The moment when couples arrive at the altar can be tense, but all took a deep breath, joined hands and relaxed.

I began, "Dearly beloved, we are gathered here . . .-"

It might be more interesting if somebody fainted, or a jealous boyfriend disrupted the service, but the ceremony went without a hitch. They stammered through the traditional vows. And although the blood drained from the groom's face once or twice, and his hands were clammy when he slipped the ring on her finger, all went smoothly. When it was time to kiss the bride, the veil gave him a run for his money. Pictures were taken, until the flash batteries died. The best man and maid of honor signed the legal papers, and all joined the guests at the reception.

The bride's mother had baked and brought the wedding cake in the back of the family station wagon from some distance. A lovely piece of art, with three tiers, and all covered with Mother's famous seven-minute icing. However, seventy-two hours or more had passed since then. Time, distance and weather had turned the icing into something akin to aluminum siding. When the bride and groom sliced

The Wedding

the cake, their two hands as one, the icing cracked and slipped like snow sliding off a roof.

No one minded. The bride laughed, the groom looked at her as though she were a Greek goddess, and parents smiled and wept. The event had character.

One might have thought that the marriage had little chance of survival. Surely one or the other would wake up some day and wonder, *what made me think I wanted to spend the rest of my life with you?* That didn't happen.

For many years they sent us family pictures on Christmas cards. Babies appeared and grew into young men and women, and there were more weddings. I wish I could have attended them. Who knows . . . maybe I would have helped shake the wrinkles from a veil, or smiled over icing too brittle to slice. It had worked for their parents. What more could they have possibly wished for themselves? In time we lost contact.

Recently, after many years, I returned to Drumright, where I had performed this wedding, and stood at the back of the sanctuary greeting folks. A couple approached and she said, "You probably don't remember, but forty years ago you married us in this church. My name was Radabaugh . . . ."

Theirs had truly been a storybook marriage.

KIDS AND CARS

WHEN DO PREACHERS BUY A NEW CAR? When he is about to move. Merchants in your church figures they've helped pay your salary and you should trade with them. No problem with that for goods or food, but a car is different. The local Chevrolet dealer will expect you to buy from him, but if you are packing to leave, and don't care for Chevys, you can choose a different make and it won't have a lasting impact. When you arrive at your new destination the local dealer-member doesn't expect you to trade in a brand new car.

Just before we moved to Aldersgate UMC in Tulsa, I bought a new Mazda. It was a sporty version and promised good mileage.

That fall our Tulsa Hale High School daughter Sherri took part in the school's international student exchange program, the American Field Service. Yearly a number of kids from overseas were brought to Oklahoma, and several local youths traveled to some other country for a semester or a year. That term, one of the AFS foreign students, Chris Goertz, was from Germany. One of his high school teachers, a member of the Tulsa Opera chorus, gave him two

Kids and Cars

tickets to the Saturday night performance and the cast party following. Chris invited our daughter to go with him, but he was not allowed to drive in the United States. We would need to provide transportation. Sherri wanted to drive and not be embarrassed by her dad taking them. She had turned sixteen that July and had gotten her license, but was not yet seasoned behind the wheel.

I was nervous, so I insisted she drive a test route that afternoon to downtown Tulsa, the opera house, and past the Mayo hotel where the cast party would be held. She did well.

On Saturday night I was in my church study about 10:30, working on my sermon. The phone rang. It was Paula, in a panic. A phone call had come from a man who said, "Ma'am, someone gave me this number to call. There has been an accident at Second Street and Cincinnati. The ambulance is here." He hung up.

I called the police department and was told an ambulance had been cleared from that intersection to the ER at Hillcrest Hospital. On the way Paula and I tried to convince ourselves that if Sherri was conscious enough to give someone our phone number, she was okay. But what about her passenger Chris?

We arrived at the hospital to discover there had been a second car wreck, and a person hurt in that incident had been brought to the ER, under police escort. They were guarding all entrances to the treatment rooms. We could not get to the kids. A couple we knew from Christ UMC were serving there as a care team for persons waiting in the emergency room.

They were able to slip in to check on Sherri and Chris and reported both were fine, with just a few cuts.

The daylight trial run had not taken into account the difference of night driving. Sherri had run a red light and a Cadillac broadsided the Mazda – rolling it one and a half times, landing against a building – upside down. Apparently, just before the impact, Chris had seen the approaching Cadillac, and passed out. His only injury came when the emergency people cut the seatbelt and he fell onto the car floor, cutting his head on broken glass. Sherri also needed a few stitches. Still, we had to call Chris' parents in Germany to tell them what had happened and assure them their son was fine.

My new car, however, was totaled.

Sherri felt bad that she had destroyed it, but we assured her that the most important thing was, she was okay. I could get another car.

This time I bought a big heavy Ford LTD, thinking it would provide better protection for two teenagers learning to drive.

A week later, in the LTD with son Artie, I was driving on the inside lane. As I passed a shopping center, the driver on my right slowed and motioned a car exiting the parking lot to proceed. It smashed into my right front fender, knocking the bumper loose. The man who had signaled the driver, backed up, drove around and sped away. We got out and surveyed the damage. Artie tried to lift the bumper so we could drive, but it fell on his foot, mashing a toe. The only business in sight was a bar, but they had a phone and we waited there until Paula picked

Kids and Cars

us up. The car wasn't ruined, but it spent time in the repair shop.

Sherri teased that it wasn't necessary for me to do that so she would feel better – but she did.

Son Art had no big wrecks just small ones, mostly involving immovable objects. On the day I took him for his driver's test he was worried about parallel parking. Ahead on the street, a lone car sat at the curb. I told him to use it as a last practice. He pulled alongside – backed smoothly in a perfect maneuver.

"You did fine. Let's go for that exam."

He put the car in gear and ran smack into the car behind which he had just parked.

On one occasion he swerved to miss a parked car that he hadn't noticed was sitting still, careened across the street, up into a yard and knocked down a small tree. Later, this asthmatic son confessed he was trying to retrieve a lit cigarette he had dropped on the floorboard.

Another time in a store parking lot he let his car roll into the one in front of him – crinkling a fender. Same story – dropped cig.

By then I had bought a second car, a used Datsun 510. Except for its bright yellow paint, this car was plain. It had an AM radio, no stereo, and the air conditioner worked fine provided the outside temperature wasn't more than 85 degrees. Art thought I should put a tape player in it, but such skills were not in my personal tool kit, and we couldn't afford to have one installed.

Artie said, "My buddy, Steve, does this kind of thing all the time to his family's cars. He can install it and I can help and learn how."

How could I resist?

On Saturday morning they drove my car away with the promise it would only take a couple of hours to complete. Three hours passed – then four – five.

Art called. "We're having a little difficulty, but we think it'll be done soon."

At six o'clock, Art came home with no Datsun 510. The *difficulty* turned out to be a hole in the steel brake line under the floorboard, which they had *accidently* punctured while installing the tape player. For most of the day they'd searched parts stores, dealerships and junk yards, seeking a replacement. They discovered that, for this model, the s*teel* line had to be special ordered – from Japan.

Time has erased my memory of the total cost of the gas line, plus the air-shipping charges from Tokyo, but it likely would have paid for the installation of an entire *stereo surround sound system*.

Or perhaps the price was worth the kidding I gave Art and Steve – for years.

SWEET REVENGE

OUR CHURCH OFFICE NEEDED PAINTING. As usual the budget was in no condition to have it done by professionals. So, Steve, the president of the Aldersgate men's group, and Bob, his across-the-street neighbor, volunteered to do the job, and provide the paint. They would take the weekend to complete the project. It did not occur to me that I should check in on them. They worked without interruption and completed the job early Saturday afternoon.

The extra time brought out a streak of playfulness. One of them suggested that my office needed more than fresh paint. It needed new décor and he knew just where to get it—from the bookstore of the local famed evangelist, Oral Roberts.

They knew he was not among my favorite religious figures. Arming themselves with banners, slogans, pictures and icons, they made my office look as though I was Oral's number one fan.

Sunday morning, I was greeted with a display that would have made P.T. Barnum proud. Even if I hadn't known who the perpetrators were, it would have been apparent when they arrived. They could barely contain themselves. I waited to see if a confession by way of over-eager questions would be forthcoming. Sure enough, one of them, barely stifling a wide grin asked, "Preacher, how did you like the new office look?"

I replied, "It was nice. Thanks for your hard work." Acknowledging that it was a real work of art, I let it go at that.

Taking some kidding about my feelings toward the evangelist seemed little enough pay for the fresh paint. Still, it was not my nature to let something like this pass without a response.

That week an article had appeared in the local paper about a bizarre incident in Dallas, Texas. For Labor Day Sunday an Episcopal priest had invited his church members to demonstrate a hobby or what they did for a living. Several normal offerings were shared – needlepoint, woodworking, someone wrote poetry. But there was in that congregation a young woman who made her living as a strip tease artist. She proposed a demonstration on Sunday, and the priest agreed. The house was packed.

I knew how I would respond to my two painters. The men's club was to begin meeting after taking the summer off. It was customary for fall's first event to be a special program.

Our weekly church paper carried a message from the pastor on the front page. Sometimes it was inspirational, at other times an announcement of some upcoming event.

I wrote a lead article to promote the first meeting of the men's club. Then I wrote a second version designed to fit in the same space. It told of the young

Sweet Revenge

stripper who had displayed her wares at her church in Dallas, and announced that Steve, our president of the men's club, had secured her services for their first meeting. His neighbor Bob would introduce her. The article explained that everyone who wanted to attend should call the president to make reservations. I printed only two copies of the second rendition and substituted them for the papers going only to my erstwhile decorators.

Early the next evening, my phone rang. "You . . . you . . . "Steve stammered, "p-p-preacher, you didn't send this to everyone, did you?"

Both men had picked up the church paper at about the same time. Each exploded from his house simultaneously. They met in the middle of the street. They were convinced it must have been sent to the whole church. After a bit of banter, I assured them they had the only copies.

It could have stopped there, but being good sports, they thought it worthy of passing along to the whole church.

Oh, sweet revenge.

THE VEXERS

SOME CHURCHES, AFTER YEARS OF RUNNING off multiple preachers, are labeled *killer congregations*. Thankfully these are rare. Fortunate is the pastor never assigned to one.

In general, Methodist folk esteem their ministers. They sometimes endure less than polished preachers, or *grow up young ones*, and hope for improvement with each new assignment. No one stays forever.

But there are congregations with individuals for whom the new pastor, from day one, just isn't a fit. Some miss their departed spiritual advisor so deeply they won't give the new one a chance. A few, however, develop the reputation of hassling *every* preacher who comes their way.

I call them *the vexers*.

Days after I arrived at the Aldersgate church, Bob the Lay Leader, came by to bid me welcome. After some polite banter he probed my attitudes on several subjects. What was my opinion about a current movement known as Liberation Theology? Did I have concerns regarding the United Methodist Publishing House and our Church School Literature, and did I think it had communist leanings? Had the General

Board of Social Concerns overstepped its authority with recent public pronouncements? My responses, however, were not the ones he wanted to hear.

The first church board meeting was a week away and he asked if there was anything I would like presented. Perplexed, I asked what he meant. At Official Board meetings I was used to giving a pastor's report.

"In this church, if the pastor wants the board to approve something, he is to first share it with me as the Lay Leader – and if I consider it worthwhile, I will present it."

I told him that I had been appointed by the bishop as the *minister in charge* and that I preferred speaking directly to the leadership. I offered to discuss with him any proposals I was contemplating, but claimed my role as pastor to present them. All pretense of friendliness faded – his eyes narrowed, his smile disappeared, and he coldly said, "Well, nothing you ask for will ever get approved!"

Nice beginning, I thought. *I've alienated the leading lay person of the congregation.*

At the first board meeting I had no requests so his threat was not tested. Later, his claim proved empty as the leaders gladly received my suggestions and acted positively on many. He was bluffing.

A few weeks went by, and all seemed to be going well until Bob again dropped in to talk. He presented me with a list of changes he claimed I'd made in the order of worship, none of which he had been consulted about, nor approved. Over the sermons I had preached he had counted how few times I had spoken the word *Jesus*. I learned that he had not counted the phrase, *Jesus Christ*. He thought that too formal.

In a new assignment, most pastors know not to abruptly change the format of the worship service. I assured him I had made none. He was certain of his observations yet refused when I offered to go to the church files and compare the previous year's bulletins with ones since I had arrived.

He was a master of the "why don't you two fight" tactic. He would plant counter thoughts with two people. In a board meeting he would raise a seemingly innocent question calculated to bait his two *plants* to argue. Soon the board was in an uproar. Bob sat back and smiled. He had killed any positive action that night.

I learned from some former youth sponsors that before I arrived, Bob had taken them aside to warn them that I would destroy the youth department. Since I had two youth of my own in that age group I wondered why on earth he thought I would want to do that.

I had several conversations with Bob as I attempted to understand his motives and why he seemed so dead-set against my leadership.

Once he asked me where the two pastors I followed had attended seminary. We had all graduated from Perkins School of Theology at Southern Methodist University. He said, "How come each of you came out of the same school with such different ideas?" I told him that graduate school had taught us *how* to think, not *what*.

The Vexers

On one occasion, he gave me an insight into his inner struggles. He shared that his mother had pushed him to go into ministry, but he had become an engineer instead. Perhaps his conflicts with preachers were a reaction to bucking his mother's wishes

I gathered a small group of persons I felt were open to calmly discussing issues of the church and seek creative solutions. We met often and enjoyed one another's company, as we worked on matters of importance. They filtered these ideas into the board meetings without them appearing to come from me. Bob was distraught and, for a time, could not figure out my end runs.

My frustration with him grew and in one of our small group sessions I bewailed my anguish. When I paused in my whine, one of the men said, "Why don't you let us take care of Bob? If you will back off, we'll figure out a way to dull his negativity."

I agreed.

Over the next months the group quietly isolated Bob – not to run him off, but to lessen his destructiveness. By the end of my second year he resigned as the Lay Leader.

Some years after we left, we were invited back for the church's twenty-fifth anniversary. I was determined to avoid Bob, unsure if I could keep my remarks civil, and I had nothing to gain by a confrontation.

At the luncheon following church, I went to refresh our drinks and, turning a corner, came face-to-face with Bob.

He stuck out his hand. "David, I was hoping I would get to see you."

We shook, as I pondered what to say to him.

"I wanted to tell you, if I got the chance, that I realize I gave you a bad time when you were here. I'm sorry for what I did. In fact, you were one of the best pastors this church has ever had."

I silently reflected he must have truly disliked the ministers that followed me, but decided to be gracious in turn, thanked him and went back to my seat in a daze.

Even vexers can change.

THE INVITATION

THE PHONE CALL CAME AT THE RIGHT MOMENT. It had been two rough years as pastor of Tulsa's Aldersgate. We had arrived to find a group of successful young adults, but from non-United Methodist backgrounds, had captured the leadership positions in the congregation. Their basic belief understanding was informed by a millennialist theology school in Dallas, Texas – of the *"Late Great Planet Earth"* flavor. Some carried *rapture robes* with them in eager expectation of the imminent end of the world, although none had cancelled their home-owners or life insurance policies. All United Methodist Sunday school literature had been removed from the children and youth departments, and replaced with ultra-conservative David C. Cook materials. In their Sunday school class, they listened to fundamentalist audio tapes. They didn't mind informing us long-time Methodist folk, that we were *biblical nincompoops*.

All of this had not been disclosed to me by Dr. Dorff, my District Superintendent and, several months into my tenure when my frustration peaked, I went to his office to ask him why I hadn't been informed about the condition of the church. He responded, "We thought you were the person to turn the church back into a United Methodist congregation!" It would have been nice to know that. It was as though he thought, if he had given me a *heads up,* I might have refused to accept the appointment.

In many ways these young adults were wonderful, but clearly had no interest in a change of their understanding. Slowly we began to replace them with United Methodist leaders. We decided to try to "love them into new thinking, or, if not, hope they would leave quietly." We didn't want a sudden mass exodus. Over the next year, most quietly slipped away to churches that supported their theological mindset. And they took their tithes with them, leaving our congregation financially crippled.

I was battle weary. The phone call was well timed.

"Would you be interested in joining the staff of the General Board of Health and Welfare Ministries?"

With no hesitation, I said yes.

"Will you and your wife come to Evanston, Illinois, to be interviewed?"

"Yes, of course."

Some days later we landed at O'Hare International in Chicago, rented a car, and found our way to the headquarters building on Davis Street in Evanston.

I had led our Oklahoma Annual Conference Health and Welfare Board in expanding its ministries. The National Association of Health and Welfare Conference meeting, recognizing those accomplishments, had bestowed on me their "Outstanding Conference Board Chair Award." Paula took time off from school and flew to Atlanta to be there along with

The Invitation

other leaders of our local committee, Jim Wheeler, Paul Bowles, Carl Cartwright and Don Johnson. I felt a deep appreciation for being recognized.

It was a good time to consider the invitation to lead at the national level of our church. Paula's only concern was that at our kids' high-school age, it might not be a good idea.

I made an appointment to see Bishop Millhouse to tell him I was considering accepting the invitation.

However, there was a problem with housing. We had lived in parsonages most of our married life, and now would need to buy a house or rent one. We doubted a housing allowance would cover that expense. It also meant we must purchase furniture which, up to this point, had been provided by the churches we served.

Before we left for the interview we visited several Tulsa furniture stores. The first question the sales clerks asked was, "What style of furniture are you interested in?" We didn't know. When you itinerate, you take what is there. Since church-owned houses are often filled with items church members no longer wanted, we called it, *Early American Parsonage Style*. The store clerk didn't know that design.

After the interview and invitation to join the General Board staff, we began house hunting in and around Evanston. Our realtor asked questions as well. "What style of house do you like?" Four walls and a non-leaky roof didn't narrow it much. The more serious question was what could we afford? "Not much!" Anything in or near the city was well out of our price range. The realtor continued driving west. Each time we went through a new village and saw a United Methodist Church, I thought, *I wonder if I could teach a Sunday school class there.*

Finally, we found what we thought we could afford and made a low-ball offer, even though it meant a daily long rush-hour drive to and from the office. Looking back, I think Paula and I both hoped they would reject our bid.

We boarded the plane back to Tulsa and my seatmate turned out to be a man who was, shall we say, a *lapsed Methodist*. When he found out I was a preacher he wanted to tell me why he no longer attended his church. I began offering him suggestions to consider, options to try, counter arguments to his paper-thin excuses. For the hour and a half flight, we talked, and when we deplaned he thanked me for listening to him and promised to try a different church than the one he had been working so hard to stay away from.

As we walked down the corridor toward the baggage claim, Paula squeezed my hand and said, "You aren't going, are you?"

I took a few steps, then said, "No, no sweetheart, I'm not. I want to be in the local church. I want to be a pastor. Let's go home."

MAYFAIR MEMORIES

IN MY SIXTH POST-SEMINARY APPOINTMENT WE moved to Oklahoma City and Mayfair Heights UMC. I knew this assignment would be fun when I found a membership list left by my predecessor, Marvin. A red dot marked the names of families who would help me fulfill Paul's admonition in I Timothy 5:23 to "take a little wine for your stomach."

Before my first Sunday I met with Tommy Roberson, the chair of the Pastor Parish Committee. He told me that in the summer the dress code was informal. Men did not wear suits or ties. I was more comfortable in a suit for my first service. We hit on a plan.

Sunday morning I wore a dress shirt and an old tie. When Tommy introduced Paula and me he said, "I told David we were very informal here in the summer." He pulled out a pair of long scissors and whacked off my tie just below the knot. The congregation gasped. I said nothing and led the service with the stub in place. After church several people apologized for Tommy's behavior, and a couple of men offered to replace my cut-off cravat. Although we tried to assure everyone it was a pre-arranged deal, many did not believe us. When I left, five years later, some still thought Tommy had been out of line.

The sanctuary at Mayfair Heights had a modern high A-frame style ceiling. The room was light and bright. The windows, only two feet high, ran the length of the sanctuary at the top of the east and west walls. The panes were colored but not stained glass.

One Spring Mike Gleason, a young CPA, spoke during Joys and Concerns and expressed his delight at being past the crunch of tax season and getting back to church. A week later while driving home on the yet-to-be completed Hefner Parkway, a car turned down the wrong side of the road and hit Mike's car head-on, killing him instantly. It was a shattering blow to the church, especially his Sunday school class. They rallied around his family and, for many of them, faced the first major death event in their lives. The outpourings of memorial gifts provided the opportunity to redo the sanctuary windows in his memory.

A committee from the Trustees and Mike's young adult class was formed. They accepted my idea of a series of scenes depicting Bible stories, and Methodist and Evangelical Brethren heritage panels. An Oklahoma City faceted-glass artist was commissioned to create the work.

Beginning with the southeast corner window, the artist created panels of Old Testament, then New Testament scenes. Along the west side of the building, starting at the back of the room, she designed windows showing early Methodist history, then Evangelical United Brethren, then the United

Methodist and Mayfair church, ending in a futuristic window at the south-west corner. To show the encompassing of God's spirit, the artist created an outstretched hand in the first window with a red line flowing from it through each panel, and ending in the last window in the southwest corner with another hand. God's care proceeds from the past on into the unknown future.

Our pipe organ was woefully underpowered for the size of the sanctuary. We learned that the Bristow UMC had purchased a new instrument and wanted to sell their old one, which was more than twice the size. We bought it and engaged a craftsman to rebuild and install it.

A special celebration concert was planned. I invited the organist from St. Luke's UMC to be the guest artist. He came during the week before to practice and was not impressed with our new acquisition. He complained loudly that it was of poor quality and implied it was beneath him to even be asked to play it. His concert was lousy. He played a few numbers and quit. Clearly our purchase had been a major mistake.

We had spent a lot of money on this project, and for days I mourned our error. Late in the week a young man, a pre-ministry student at Bethany Nazarene College, came to inquire about our new pipe organ. I told him it wasn't new, but rebuilt, and feared it wasn't very good. He asked to see it, sat at the console and fiddled with the stops awhile. Then he struck a chord and began to play. The music was heavenly. It sounded nothing like the concert the previous Sunday evening. After several minutes I asked him, "Are you looking for a job?" He was, and became our organist until he graduated from college. What a blessing.

J. L. and Betty Sanders became great friends. He owned a pawn shop and was our regular greeter Sunday mornings. When I was to go to San Francisco on a church trip I planned to take Paula. We mentioned it to the Sanders and they wanted to go with us. We left a few days before my meeting and toured from San Francisco to Bodega Bay, then inland through the Redwoods, Napa wine country and back to the city. Although they were several years our senior, we had to hustle to keep up with them, especially around Fisherman's Wharf.

J. L. and Betty loved to pull funny stunts. They had a friend who was entertaining company from some far-off non-Okie state. The Sanders dressed as country hicks and dropped in on them for a visit. After embarrassing their friends, they decided to come tell us what they had done. The doorbell rang and I welcomed them. I had just returned from the airport with a gentleman from our New York General Board of Global Ministries, our United Methodist missions' agency. Getting behind J. L., I ushered him into our den and guided him around a chair to face our guest. As he realized what was happening he tried to back up, but I introduced him as one of our leading laymen in the church.

Every church has financial problems, and Mayfair Heights was no exception. A popular fundraising method was selling church bonds. They were sold mainly to church members. They earned the interest, and the church funded its projects.

Mayfair had a bond program, but it was with a company who designed them for younger growing congregations. Anticipating a rapid increase in members, the annual payment increased each year. Our static-growth church couldn't keep up.

In three months, the next payment was due and it was clear there wouldn't be enough cash on hand. I asked the church treasurer to go to the bank and bring me $500 in twenty-dollar bills. The following Sunday I preached on the Parable of the Talents and offered a Jackson to anyone who would take it and multiply it in the next six weeks. The congregation responded well. Some baked and sold food – some bought yarn and knitted items. At the end of the six weeks everyone brought back their gains.

Colonel McAfee, Ret., who had served in the Pentagon JAG section, gave me an envelope with about $200 in it, and remarked, "Don't ask me how I did it." Someone told me he was known for gambling on the golf course and probably had fleeced his golf buddies.

We were close to paying off the debt, but needed one more push. I designed a program with lapel buttons that said, "I'M FOR S-I-N. The letters stood for, STOP INTEREST NOW. It worked. We raised the money and paid off the debt.

Mayfair was a delightful assignment.

GO WHERE I SEND THEE

Rev. Dr. Bonner Teeter held a special place in Paula's and my lives. He was the dean of the West Oklahoma Conference Camp at Turner Falls in 1952 when she and I took the first tentative steps toward a relationship, and our first kiss. A few years later, when we started planning our wedding, we needed a preacher to perform the ceremony. Neither of us had a strong relationship to the current pastors of our home churches, so we went to visit Bonner, who was the pastor of First Methodist in Guthrie. He was delighted we asked him, but made one stipulation, "I'll do it, if you two will memorize the wedding vows and instead of repeating them sentence by sentence after me, say the vows to each other." We agreed. Over the years of my ministry there have been a few that accepted that challenge from me, but most were too frightened to do so.

He remained a good friend over the ensuing years as he rose in the ranks to larger churches and finally was asked to be a District Superintendent over the Ardmore District.

Now, D.S.s are supposed to keep secrets, especially being careful not to reveal someone's upcoming appointment before the Bishop said it was okay. But that was difficult for Bonner, and he was known for "spilling the beans," early.

We were at some meeting and he casually said to me, "When you get to Ada, bring your fishing pole and we will go catch some fish."

"What'd you say, Bonner?"

"I said, when you get to Ada bring your fishing pole."

"Are you trying to tell me something?"

"Maybe."

And he walked away.

That evening I stewed over his remarks and called him for further information. All I got was, "Your D.S. will come see you."

I looked up the statistics on Ada First UMC and discovered that it had fallen on hard times. Average attendance was low for a church of that size. And the salary was at least a couple of thousand a year less than what I was making. Was I being demoted? I was not pleased.

Sure enough, a few days later my D.S., Dr. Cliff Sproules called and said he wanted to drop by and visit.

When he came the conversation began with banal matters. He had no idea that I already had a hint as to why he was there. Finally, he took a deep breath and said:

"David, the Bishop would like to appoint you to Ada First Church." This he said as if it was the opportunity of a lifetime.

I said to him, "Why? Why is he demoting me? Why a pay cut? What has caused this?"

Cliff was taken aback at my question. He stammered about the salary, indicating he didn't think it was less.

I said, "Well, I would like to visit in person with Bishop Hardt. Will you get me an appointment with him?"

He agreed to do that, but several weeks passed and nothing was said, nor a time with the Bishop offered. I decided I would have to do it myself and began trying to get on his calendar.

It didn't take long to discover he wasn't very interested in having a conversation with me. After several attempts I finally got him on the phone. He listened to me briefly, but said, "David, I'm getting ready to leave for the airport to fly to Dallas."

I said, "Bishop, how about I pick you up and take you to the airport." After a long pause he agreed and I headed for his house.

We hadn't driven but a few blocks when Bishop Hardt said, "David, did I ever tell you how I was appointed to First Church Beaumont?"

"No Sir, I don't believe so."

"The year before I went there, my Bishop said, 'John Wesley, I would like you to go to First Church Beaumont next Conference. Now back then everybody knew that old downtown church was declining and had little chance to recover. I told my Bishop I wasn't interested and assumed that ended it. It didn't. Every time I'd see the him he'd bring up Beaumont. And every time I told him I wasn't interested. Finally, in the spring before Annual Conference he said he had arranged a meeting with the District Superintendent in Beaumont along with some leading lay people from First Church. 'John Wesley,' he said, 'I want you to go down there and visit with those folks, and then come back and tell me you will go there. I did and had a wonderful ministry.'"

I knew when he finished his story that in a very sweet way he was saying, "David, you're going to First Church Ada, and you will have a wonderful ministry there." And I did.

"Go where I send thee, ah yes I signed on to be sent into ministry where I was needed."

But my friend Bonner moved the next year, and he never did take me fishing.

MOSES LEANED ON HIS STAFF AND DIED
(Paraphrasing Genesis 47:31)

PASTORS USUALLY BEGIN THEIR CAREERS IN small-membership churches – with no staff. You open and close the building, arrange chairs, make coffee, and clean up whatever messes are left.

Personnel are added as you progress in the size and complexity of churches. Then you become a boss and realize that, in seminary, nobody told you about managing staff. It's *on-the-job training*.

In the first church I served, where there was staff, I learned *how not* to manage when an employee is dismissed.

The personnel committee determined that we needed a full-time secretary. The part-time person didn't want to work full time, and resigned. I asked her if she could stay on until we found someone. Big mistake. She instigated maneuvers to reverse the full-time decision. She had performed most tasks at a pokey pace now they were done *pronto*. She would ask me for additional tasks to do, because, "There just doesn't seem to be that much work in this office." My complaints of misspelled words in the worship bulletin had never gotten through to her. Now I was being asked to proof her work. She became a paragon of efficiency, accompanied by little remarks on *how well she was doing*. I received calls from her church buddies who wondered why on earth we would replace *such a fine employee*. The callers repeated verbatim the secretary's phrase about not enough work to be done.

It was a painful three weeks before we replaced her.

When a staff person must be dismissed, it best be done quickly. Give them a nice severance check, throw a little party, and bid them "God speed." And take their keys.

In some places a staff change should have been done prior to my arrival, but wasn't.

A few weeks before we were to move to Ada, we were visited by Carl, the vice-chair of the Staff-Parish Committee. They hire and fire.

We learned some things about the new community and the congregation. Then, as he stood to leave, he uttered one of the most dreaded phrases preachers hear, *Oh by the way*. He said, "When you get there you'll have to fire the choir director."

I asked him to sit back down and explain.

Carl related that the out-going minister had accused the choir director of swiping his sermon notes from the pulpit. The offense was denied, but a kerfuffle followed and the backers of the pastor prevailed on the Pastor Parish Committee to act. Of course, they didn't, but decided they would ask the incoming pastor to oust the choir director.

I protested to the bearer of this good news that their request would start me off on the wrong foot. It would be best to fire that person before I arrived.

We moved in to discover that no firing had taken place. Instead, the committee planned to announce at the upcoming board meeting the following Wednesday, that the position was to be immediately down-graded to half-time, anticipating the young man would resign. If their recommendation was accepted the young man would be forced out on short notice. That didn't seem fair.

On Friday before my first Sunday service, I was unpacking books in my office. A steady stream of well-wishers dropped by. About half said something like, "I'm sorry you'll be present for a contentious board meeting, but they're trying to get rid of our wonderful choir director, and we're not going to let that happen." The other half said it was necessary to let the choir director go, even though a *few folks* were not happy about it.

Nothing like being the captain of the Titanic, headed for the iceberg.

Sunday services went well. I was hoping to visit with Roy, the Chair of the Pastor-Parish Committee, but he wasn't in church. On Monday morning the choir director invited me to his service club luncheon. On the way back to the office I asked him how he felt about the impending meeting.

He said he was worried he was about to lose his job, but was getting a lot of support from choir members and some congregants. He didn't know what to do.

I had to share what I felt. I told the young man, who was in his first job after graduating from Choir College, that I thought he might win the battle next week but felt, in the long-run, he would lose the war. Then I said, "Do you want to run the risk of your being fired from your first job, rather than resigning? It might not look good on your resume."

He hadn't thought of that.

A plan came to mind. "I am not asking you to resign," I said. "If you don't want to, that's okay. However, if you think that it might be best for *your* future, I will do my best to convince the committee to keep you on and give you the next three months to look for new employment."

Back at the church he went to his office to contemplate. In a little while he knocked on my door.

"I don't know how to write a letter of resignation."

I helped him frame his message, indicating the decision was his alone. I asked him to bring me three copies. I took two of them, and instructed him to go visit the president of the choir and give her the third.

The following day the Chair of the Pastor-Parish Committee asked me to lunch. We chit-chatted during the meal until he finally got around to the choir director. He told me about the conflict between the pastor and the director, and the proposed action of the committee.

Before he went further, I reached into my coat pocket and brought out the letter and handed it to Roy saying, "Maybe you should read this."

He read it – looked up and said, "How the *hell* did you get this?" I said I had a request of the committee.

Rather than the motion they were prepared to make would they meet and accept his resignation, with appreciation, and approve him staying on, at his full salary, until the end of August. Roy agreed and the committee followed.

Instead of a contentious firing, the board meeting turned out to be a love-fest.

The young man did find a new job and for several years we stayed in touch as he progressed from church to church.

Now, not all my staff *partings* were that successful, oh no!

Why, I could tell you . . . .

BE CAREFUL WHAT
YOU WISH FOR

A WISE PERSON ONCE SAID, "BE CAREFUL what you wish for, you just might get it!" So it was with my appointment to First Church Edmond. I had long wanted to serve there and when Bishop John Wesley Hardt appointed me, I was elated.

The city of Edmond had been booming for years. New housing developments sprung up like dandelions and the population had exploded to over 50,000. It was no longer the sleepy college town of my childhood memory and through which my family traveled on rare trips to Oklahoma City. Some said the growth was due to white flight, or fear of inner city school problems, or was the inevitable expansion from Oklahoma City.

However, soon after arrival I discovered a few unsettling things. The church building was old, and much in need of renovation. The plastered walls of the sanctuary had holes all the way to the slat work. Parking was limited and not conducive to attracting new visitors, the main entrance a steep set of stairs. They could seat around 200 comfortably, a great vision in the day in which they had built the church, but not adequate now.

A series of small home meetings were set up for me to listen to the congregation's vision for its future. An unnerving number expressed limited hope or desire for growth, and some still imagined the population of the city was around the 8,000 people of many generations before.

A family life building, less than two years old, had a payment of more than $40,000 due within a short time.

The treasurer had not returned my calls and, if he was in worship, didn't identify himself. I finally ran into him at a reception one Sunday evening.

"I've been trying to reach you."

"I've been avoiding you," he said.

I asked why.

"I didn't want to tell you we don't have the money to make the building payment."

"What about the sinking fund? You know you're required by law to deposit an amount weekly that will cover each semi-annual installment?"

He replied, "We needed the money to pay bills and salaries." And he went on to explain that this wasn't the first time. They had borrowed funds to make the previous installment as well.

When there wasn't enough in the reserve fund, the money for that payment had been provided by a church member who, we later learned, loaned the funds from his company's pension reserves. It wasn't long before I received a call saying that it must be paid back immediately, as they'd learned it wasn't exactly legal. No kidding.

Within days of arriving I knew the church was faced with raising three semi-annual debt installments, with little hope of doing so. It meant that the debt on the building which had originally been around $750,000 was now closer to a million. Some members wondered how I had managed to spend all that money in so short a time.

The second blow came when the treasurer informed me that he also had to pay current bills using most of the funds that had been deposited by the parents of our pre-school students to pre-register their child for the fall. In a little over two months those funds would be required.

A few weeks prior to our moving to Edmond my District Superintendent called to offer me a choice between two persons to be our associate pastor. Some awareness of the church's financial straits had already reached my ears, although I had no idea how serious. I expressed surprise that an associate would be appointed. There already was an associate and some other staff so, given the conditions, I didn't expect the second position to be filled. The D.S. insisted that the church leaders had not told the Cabinet otherwise and they would be sending someone. My only choice was which of the two I wanted. Looking back on the mutiny I clearly made the wrong choice.

Thanks to the loyalty of the congregation we made it. We found a new church bond program that eased the building payments and the members came through with the money needed to replace the preschool funds.

The following two years were rocky, including my almost having to move. But in the end, we had a good ministry there and knew many loving and caring church folks.

QUARRELSOME SAINTS AND PARKING LOT SUMMITS

EVERY CHURCH I SERVED HAD WONDERFUL parishioners who loved the church and their pastor. But sometimes there were those who created conflict. Dealing with people who thrive on turmoil requires tact, insight, and grace, qualities not easy to acquire, let alone maintain. My record was spotty, at best.

Soon after moving to Ada, a local dentist dropped by my office to say, "Preacher, I don't believe any thing ought to be decided by a unanimous vote. In a Board meeting you can count on me to vote no because every issue should have a contrary opinion." He kept his word. No matter how positive an outcome seemed, Doc voted no.

That same week Mr. Richardson, an automobile dealer, came by. His warm spirit put me at ease. "Preacher, I have loved every pastor that has been here, and I'll love you. I hope your years with us will be a time of joy in your life."

While examining the financial books in another church I discovered an entry, dated almost a decade before, marked New Church Sign. No sign existed in front of the church. The Church Treasurer said the funds had been provided by an individual, now deceased. The Chair of the Trustees said the issue was whether the sign should be set horizontally or vertically and, every time it was discussed an argument broke out and the matter was tabled. Finally, the funds and the intended sign were forgotten.

Some churches have the DNA of being difficult and one congregation was widely known as quarrelsome.

It was a church in far northwest Oklahoma and had the reputation of not being the easiest group to get along with, although we had wonderful friends there, I learned about a tactic I would run into in other congregations. I call it *the parking-lot summit*. The church board takes a vote approving some matter. After the meeting a handful of old timers huddle in the parking lot and determine not to accept the action. The next day a call came.

"*We decided* we aren't gonna do that."

And *we didn't*.

Years after serving there, Paula and I attended their 100th anniversary celebration. The bulletin listed the preachers and the years they'd served. In a century they had received, and often ran off, forty-nine preachers. I had stayed four years myself, meaning some hadn't lasted a year. I returned the second year, unconvinced of the congregation's psychosis. The third year I went back, certain I could win them over – and the fourth year to prove they couldn't run me off. Big mistake. When we moved I took an ulcer with me.

In one community a small group of lay people wanted to explore a deeper spiritual faith journey. About a dozen committed to a mid-week early morning prayer and bible study. However, in a small community people are wary of out-of-the norm activities. Soon concerns were raised, questions asked, and fears expressed about what that group was up to, anyway. A clutch of people, mostly middle aged, asked me to meet with them, hoping to put a stop to whatever we were doing.

I tried to explain and be understanding, but did not agree with them that the group was in any way detrimental to the church. I remained calm during their inquisition, but when the meeting was over, knew they had left dissatisfied. The grown daughter of one of the attendees called me the next day to share that her parents had come home in a huff. Her mother had said, "That's just great – they have taught him not to lose his temper."

My colleagues know it isn't always easy to follow a long-tenured pastor. Leadership in place may not take kindly to the new minister, even if the congregation is ready for a change. Out of a misplaced allegiance to the departed pastor, those in control take issue with everything the new preacher initiates. Their attitude might be described as, "You are the reason my preacher left me."

Such was the case in one church where, after a little over two years, the Pastor-Parish committee, who does such things, voted to ask that I be moved. No specific complaint was given and they offered no opportunity to discuss whatever was bothering them.

Fortunately, the Bishop refused to comply, and met with the committee. After visiting with him, they reversed their vote. He told me later, "David, if I had let them run you off, they would do the same to the next preacher, and the next one."

The attempt to have me moved had been kept from the congregation at large and when word got out, there was a backlash against the committee. In time, life smoothed out and the last two and a half years were most enjoyable.

During my final year there, I visited a man in the hospital who had been a member of the committee that voted for me to leave. I had learned to rely on his wise counsel as did the whole congregation.

As I was about to go he said, "David, I have been meaning to talk with you. These last two years the church has been doing well, and I know it wasn't always that way. Do you know why I think things are so much better?"

I replied, "No, Charlie, I don't, but I sure enjoy it. Why has it been so good?"

"Because, through all that bad time, you never lost your temper, you never scolded, you just loved us. Your sermons never showed any animosity toward any of us. Finally, that changed us."

I said thank you and assured him how deeply his words comforted me.

There is a sweetness about those saints who love their pastor, no matter what. But there is a special joy when someone who once opposed you becomes your friend.

Do I hear an Amen?

DESERT STORM WEDDING

My phone rang. A young man, whom I had seen in the company of a young lady of our congregation, was calling. Could they come see me?

A Marine reservist, he had been called up for Operation Desert Storm. He would be deployed in less than two weeks. They'd planned to marry the following summer, but now it seemed urgent to move up the date. *Would I marry them?*

Weary of performing marriages that lasted less than a year or two, I had resolved not to do a ceremony unless the couple first agreed to several counseling sessions. When strangers came to the church and demanded I marry them on the spot, I refused, and felt pretty righteous about it.

But what do you say to a young couple wanting to marry before he goes off to a war from which he might not return? How could I impose my rules on them when their lives were being uprooted? When I told them of my requirement their faces fell.

I said I would defer the rule if they took a pre-marital testing instrument now and left it with me. And if they'd promise to come in and discuss it when he got back, I would perform the marriage. They agreed.

Two days before he was to ship out, families and a few friends gathered at the church. The groom and groomsmen – stalwart young Marines – wore crisp khakis. The bride and bridesmaids wore simple dresses.

The ceremony went well – almost. As they knelt to recite the Lord's Prayer, I placed one hand on his shoulder and one on hers. We were no further into the prayer than, *Thy will be done* when I felt his shoulder press against my hand. By the time we got to *give us this day* it had become a decided push. I opened my eyes. He was passing out. He fell like a great redwood, slowly, silently. Finally, with a loud crash he crumpled on the chancel floor.

During my career a couple of brides had swooned. Occasionally, I thought I might lose the father of the bride at the moment of giving his daughter in marriage. Grooms always had clammy, sweaty hands, but not one had fainted.

Shortly he came around. Apparently, he had not eaten anything that day but had taken medication for a cold. As he knelt, the blood drained from his head, and the rest was predictable. All was captured on video, which the bride, no doubt, would show in future opportune times. Sheepishly, he regained his composure and stood – if a bit shaky – beside his bride. After I pronounced them husband and wife they walked out arm in arm.

After one night together, he left for the Middle East. In the midst of the war I received a letter from him telling about the raw beauty of the desert, the uniqueness of life he saw there, even in the midst of destruction. He wrote of his longing for the day when peace would rule that ancient land.

Fortunately, Operation Desert Storm didn't last long. America suffered few casualties, and our young Marine returned. They made an appointment for counseling. When they came in they surprised me.

"Would I mind doing the ceremony again?"

They would like to have another wedding and this time invite all their friends. Usually I resist redoing rituals in which we've ask God to bless a union. To repeat the rite implies that God had not done so the first time. Once again, I found myself waiving my rules.

This time the groom wore a sharp tux, and the bride a lovely wedding gown. The parents cried on cue, from relief and gratitude. And the groom made it through, as you would expect from the Marines.

Life defies our rules. Only God can say, *always* and *never*.

BATHROBES, TRUMPETS AND TIMPANIS

CHRISTMAS, MY FIRST YEAR IN EDMOND. I had read that more people return to church on Christmas Eve than any other day of the year. So, I announced to the staff that we would have Christmas Eve worship three times – at four in the afternoon for children and older folks who don't get out at night, a second at seven, plus a third at eleven o'clock.

Wes, the choir director, looked stunned. He objected, "No one will come to that late service."

A few staff heads nodded in agreement.

I said, "I think there'll be a good attendance, and we will do it."

Wes didn't give up easily. "I can't ask the choir to sing at seven and also at near midnight – we'll have to do with a soloist at eleven."

I said, "I'll talk to the choir; I think they'll be glad to."

The staff began to warm to the idea. The children's director asked, "Can we have a pageant with the kids in costumes?"

I said that was a great idea.

"Wes, there are two things that must be in a Christmas Eve service that you'll need to plan. I want a timpani and trumpets."

He reluctantly agreed.

I talked to the choir and they responded as I'd thought they would. Not only willing, they were excited.

Mary Ann Karns said, "Let's have a chili supper for the choir at my house between the two services." They began talking about who would bring what. I knew I had won.

We would have a great Christmas Eve.

There was a time when I'd held a negative opinion of what some call *bathrobe drama*. They're fraught with potential calamity – actors muff lines, or get stage fright, little ones' cry, kids stumble on long robes, Roman soldiers' trip over their wooden swords, or scenery collapses around Joseph and Mary. But it was a lead-pipe cinch to draw parents, grandparents and aunts and uncles. Besides, flubbed lines and ad-libs were the stuff of great pageantry, and theological purity is not as important as creating memories. So, aware of all the possible mishaps that might accompany such a venture – on with the show.

A few weeks out I asked Wes, "Have you found a timpani?"

As I suspected, he hadn't.

I said, "I can call Oklahoma City University and arrange to borrow one."

He mumbled, "No, I think I can get one." He did, and two trumpeters as well.

Choir rehearsals began and the pageant directors assembled the cast. Who would play Joseph and Mary, the three kings, the shepherds? A buzz stirred in the congregation.

Christmas Eve morning I sat in the sanctuary. The greenery was hung, the crèche awaited the Holy Family, but would there be a community of the faithful? Would they show?

Unsurprisingly, the afternoon service was modestly attended.

At seven o'clock the room was packed.

Had Wes been right? Would anyone come at eleven?

Ushers collected used candles and trimmed the wicks. A new batch of bulletins was laid out and we waited. By ten-forty only a handful of folks had arrived. But then a steady flow began to fill the pews. When it was time to begin, the church was full. There were even some repeats from seven o'clock. As people arrived I saw faces, whose names I didn't know.

The choir outdid themselves. The timpani's rumble underscored the bright trumpet accompaniment to *O Holy Night* which Abby Boatman's clear voice delivered flawlessly.

The children were wide-eyed-wonderful with most lines on cue. When they were to depart, one little angel lingered – unable to turn away from the child in Mary's lap. Parents and grandparents looked on through misty eyes.

We concluded with the traditional candle lighting in the darkened sanctuary. Ushers took their light from the large one I held and passed the flame down the pews. We sang *Silent Night*, and when we came to the verse, *Silent night, holy night, Son of God, love's pure light,* we lifted our flares to illumine the whole room.

Everyone filed out leaving the sanctuary shadowed, warm, and filled with expectations of the 'morrow, when we would lustily sing, *Joy to the world, the Lord is come!*

I walked down the aisle to place my candle among the others. Near the back of the sanctuary, a man sat folded in a pew, his forehead resting on the back of the one in front. He was obviously in prayer, and seemingly troubled. I sat down near him.

In a few moments he lifted his head, turned to me and said, "Preacher, I've been away too long. It's good to be here – it's great to be home."

It truly was a holy night.

CHURCH REPAIRS USING A THEOLOGY DEGREE

SEMINARY CLASSES DON'T COVER *ALL* THE skills required to be a local church pastor. I'm speaking of carpentry, plumbing, building construction, reading blueprints, heating/air conditioning repair and finances.

Systematic theology, church history and bible are important, but clergy are seriously challenged when faced with aging structures, worn out HVAC systems, leaky roofs, and flooding basements. Plus, you may have to deal with years of deferred maintenance that become unavoidable – on your watch.

In Drumright the church, an English Gothic design, leaked like a sieve. One rainy Sunday morning, as I preached, a hanging light globe slowly filled with water, a religious version of Chinese water torture.

At Tulsa and Aldersgate United Methodist. Our first Sunday we broke ground for a new education wing. Although I wasn't present during the planning, I was expected to keep a daily check on what was happening during construction. This included a shouting match with the construction foreman over a structural pole he intended to place in the middle of a classroom doorway. You learn to read blueprints!

On to Oklahoma City and Mayfair UMC. A debt issue required locating a financial group to re-do the bond program into one more viable that congregation. Shouldn't someone in the seminary have informed me I would need this skill set?

From Mayfair, we were assigned to Ada to learn that the magnificent old-world stained-glass sanctuary windows were buckling from deferred maintenance and in danger of falling out. To re-lead and restore these required $60,000 to be raised in three months. Also while there, we renovated the entire sanctuary, bought a new pipe organ, and installed a new sound system.

After Ada we landed at First UMC in Edmond, another splendid English gothic structure in need of major repair, and expansion. Because the recent building project had strapped them financially they too needed a more sensible bond program.

In most congregations I had to learn and practice skills for which I had little training. Many of my colleagues in ministry have faced these same issues. Yet, the lay people had hearts for the mission, and always proved willing and able to stretch beyond themselves to make the impossible happen.

Along the way, I have learned a few rules for the road.

1. Planning always takes longer than you *planned*.
2. It's easy to bite off more than you can chew.

3. Costs will be higher than you figured.
4. Rarely will a construction crew show up when they promise.
5. No building program was ever undertaken without some opposition.
6. No matter the project – it will take much longer than promised.
7. Some will complain, "We'll never pay for it." But they will, and sooner than they think.
8. When it is done, 90% of the congregation will be proud and pleased.

LEAVING BEFORE THE ENCORE

THE SATURDAY NIGHT OKLAHOMA CITY Philharmonic featured jazz pianist, Peter Nero. For ninety minutes Nero played the themes of Gershwin, Kern, The Beatles, Andrew Lloyd Webber, and others in the styles of Bach, Beethoven and Mozart, adding his own jazz rendition. It was a stunning performance.

As the last number ended – the audience rose in a standing ovation. But even as they applauded and cheered, dozens scurried out of the hall.

Seasoned patrons know an encore will follow a great concert. Perhaps they were Sunday School teachers and had to get home to study their lessons. Maybe babysitters went on overtime at eleven. Some in that crowd, I speculated, were unable to last a minute longer before getting a smoke, or perhaps they were driven by nature's call.

More people left, heading for the door like lemmings to the sea. Finally, I concluded they were in a rush to avoid after-show-traffic. Certain folks will always leave early. On occasion I have been among them.

While a graduate student, I attended the 1959 football game between the SMU Mustangs and the TCU Horned Frogs. Don Meredith was the quarterback for SMU. By late in the fourth quarter TCU, who had controlled the game, was ahead by almost two touchdowns. They were threatening to add another.

I headed for the car. Outside the stadium, I heard the crowd explode. I figured TCU scored. Then another roar went up. I turned on the car radio and learned an SMU defensive player had intercepted a Frog's sure TD pass and had run it back for an SMU touchdown. The second eruption came when the Mustangs recovered an on-side kick. Then Meredith unleashed one of his long bombs to his favorite receiver, Glen Gregory, and as time ran out SMU scored. They kicked the extra point and won the game 20-13. I had missed the most exciting part.

In one church Mr. Miller always sat midway in the sanctuary on the center aisle. For unknown reasons he'd concluded that nothing good happens in church after twelve noon. The preacher could be in the most dramatic moment of his sermon or the community's worst sinner repenting. At high noon Mr. Miller would don his hat, walk down the center aisle and, in a far too audible voice, announce, "Well, that's it!" Jesus could have made the Second Coming at *five after*, and Miller would have been halfway home.

Once, our daughter had a date to see *Fiddler on the Roof*. We knew it was a long movie and did not expect her home until late. We were surprised when they returned a little after ten. Because of the length of that great epic the producers had inserted an intermission, a new wrinkle in filmmaking. So, when the lights came up, they thought the movie was over, left, and missed the last half.

"We thought it had a strange ending," my daughter said.

For years I've noticed that many people leave worship during the singing of the last hymn. Nothing, not someone joining the church nor the organist's postlude, or the inspiring words of the pastor, will keep them from getting to the cafeteria ahead of the crowd or, if you live in Oklahoma, the Baptists.

What did the fleeing patrons miss the night of the Peter Nero concert? The best part of the evening. He returned to the stage, bowed, thanked the audience, and bragged on our hometown orchestra. For fifteen minutes he played an inspired encore. Every fiber of his being, every muscle and sinew became one with the music – his fingers flew over the keyboard as sure as a surgeon, as delicate as starlight.

The orchestra joined him in a rousing finale. As the last chord was struck, for the briefest moment, the music hall was silent. Then it erupted in wild, unrestrained cheers. Mr. Nero bowed and, amid thunderous applause, left the hall. We had received a rare gift. We'd all heard a superb concert performed by a gifted artist, but those who left early missed the man's soul, dancing with passion.

POLITICS, PIETY AND PROGRESS

I RETURNED TO OKLAHOMA IN 1959, AFTER seminary, as a wave of political change swept across our Conference, the governing body for Oklahoma United Methodists.

Bishop W. Angie Smith had come to Oklahoma in 1944, and would retire in 1968, having served twenty-four years – longer than anyone in our Jurisdiction.

Strong on evangelism, he stirred the clergy and laity to win people to Christ and expand Methodism in Oklahoma. He imposed new procedures for accountability from pastors for professions of faith and membership growth each year. Everyone grumbled, but complied, and churches grew. His genius was in knowing which preacher should serve what church to bring improvement to that congregation. If a church needed a new sanctuary, he knew who to send there to make it happen. It was said he knew the next three moves of every preacher, that would grow the church and promote their careers.

He gathered around him a group of clergy leaders, many former chaplains from World War II, who understood discipline and were skilled at carrying out his wishes.

Few successfully challenged Bishop Smith. He also presided over the New Mexico Annual Conference. So, if a preacher bucked the system in Oklahoma, he might find his next appointment in the Land of Enchantment.

Each four years, or quadrennium, following the General Conference, new officers were elected to lead the Annual Conference boards and agencies. For each, Bishop Smith made known his preference to be the chair. When his choice was nominated, rarely were other names offered.

However, prior to the elections of 1968, a group of us younger clergy gathered clandestinely to propose a slate of alternative leaders. I was slotted to run for the chairmanship of the Conference Board of Health and Welfare Ministries. We quietly sought support for our nominees. The results were astounding. Our *renewalist* movement captured all but two of the chair positions of the Conference. Older heads were shocked. I recall Mrs. Bess Smith, the Bishop's wife, standing in the aisle of the church, crying. She realized her husband's total control of the Conference had ended.

Some claimed this new group of young bucks brought nasty politics into the Conference. Their assumption being that the older system was free of politics and done by pious people, ordained of God and of the purest spiritual motives.

Winning was a heady experience but afterward, we gathered and asked, "What do we do now?" With leadership comes responsibility and opposition. The old guard would not give up their power so easily. Our un-thought-out plans to govern might need serious work.

The Board of Health and Welfare Ministries had oversight of children's homes, and the nursing and retirement facilities of the Conference. At the election for chair, the convening District Superintendent called for nominations and the Bishop's choice was named. Then my name was offered as well. The DS hesitated, but called for the vote. It was a tie. Fortunately, he wasn't allowed to break the impasse, and was about to call for us to vote again, when a straggler arrived. The DS looked relieved and said, "Well, good, you are just in time to break a tie between – I'm sure he didn't say it this way, but might as well have – *Bishop Smith's nominee and David Severe*."

The late-comer didn't hesitate. "I vote for David."

During the eight years I chaired, I was honored by the National Association of Health and Welfare Ministries as the Outstanding Conference Board Chair in the nation. Subsequently, I was appointed as an at-large member of the Division of Health and Welfare of the General Board of Global Ministries.

That year, 1974, at the General Conference, two petitions were received requesting the Church give special attention to the needs of persons with handicapping conditions. There was almost no mention of this subject in our Book of Discipline. One of the petitions came from Ms. Jackie Page, a quadriplegic. She was bright and capable and worked in the Mayor's office in Nashville, Tennessee. The other came from Rev. George Warren, an Oklahoma seminary student. They knew one another, but had no idea that each had submitted a proposal.

The petitions were referred to the General Board of Global Ministries for study by its Division on Health and Welfare Ministries. There, I was asked to form a committee to explore the Book of Discipline for possible changes.

We recruited people with handicapping conditions and, with others from the Division, formed the committee. I was elected chair and for two years we gathered information in all five Jurisdictions from people who shared personal stories of the pain of feeling excluded by the church or who, because of their conditions, were not even considered for ordained ministry.

Twenty-four hours before the presentation of our findings, we arranged for a number of the full-Board members to become *temporarily* handicapped. Some wore eye patches, others were confined to wheelchairs, or assumed a variety of limitations. Then the next day those with temporarily handicaps shared their experiences with the entire Board. Their testimonies were moving. Our Committee's recommendations, from accessibility guidelines for churches, to changing all Disciplinary language referring to handicapping persons, were approved to be submitted to the 1976 General Conference the following spring in Portland, Oregon.

As the elected first alternate to that conference, I was permitted to sit for clergy delegates from

Oklahoma in any Legislative Committee. Dr. John Russell, pastor at Boston Avenue in Tulsa, later to be Bishop Russell, was on the committee that would vote on our petitions. He agreed that I could replace him when our recommendations were debated.

I learned that a judge from the southeastern part of the country was vehemently opposed to what we were asking and intended to try to defeat all our proposals. I sought out the committee chair, whom I did not know, and told him the story behind our work, and asked if he would allow us to tell it before any decision was made. He agreed.

When our Disciplinary changes were introduced, the old judge jumped to his feet and moved to vote it down. The chair, true to his promise, let us speak. We shared the horror stories we had heard from people all around the country. We related the encounters of many who had been shamefully treated by the church for conditions over which they had no control. We pled for churches to be accessible, for there to be wheelchair equipped restrooms, and for Boards of Ministry not to turn down persons for ordination because they walked with a cane, or were in some way less able.

The committee began to respond favorably. An affirmative motion was made and passed overwhelmingly. Years later, Reverend Bruce Blake, who was the chair that day, became the Bishop in Oklahoma, and I was able to express my appreciation for his political and compassionate skills.

Our legislation was passed by the General Conference, and it changed our church. I am proud I had a role in that. The church became more inclusive. It opened possibilities for folks who had been left out.

It is also a tribute to how one or two people can change things for the better. Neither Jackie Page nor George Warren could have known their petitions would impact the church as much as they did. But thousands of people have had their lives enriched; their calls to ministry honored, and gained physical access to their home churches because a few people made the politics of the church work for the good of all.

Given the biblical call to do justice, it was also an act of piety.

SYSTEMS AND SATIRE

My MENTOR-PASTOR ADVISED ME, "Now, David, when you go to seminary in Dallas, keep a student church in Oklahoma. It will show your loyalty to our Conference and when you graduate you will have a leg up for a better appointment."

I finished college in May of 1956 and followed his advice. In June I became the pastor of the congregation at Springer, nestled against the south side of the Oklahoma Arbuckle Mountains.

Sherri was born in July, and in August we looked for lodging near the seminary, settling for an old servant's quarters behind the garage of a well-to-do Highland Park family. Paula, Sherri and I would commute between Dallas and Springer weekends during the school term. Summers we would be *full time,* and as it was said, *be on the charge.*

Each Friday afternoon we were off to Springer and a parsonage with no foundation and single-deck flooring. Flies, mosquitos and scorpions came and went through the cracks. The congregation was sweet but it was what it was. We endured.

I believed my home pastor understood things I did not yet know, and though the pay was terrible,

$1,500 a year – rewards would come later. I was a loyal member of our Conference. The system would take care of us.

After eighteen months in Springer we realized that the salary didn't cover our expenses. I approached my District Superintendent to request a move. I had heard that in Ardmore a church was going to need a pastor and inquired if I might be considered. The salary was double my present income. I wasn't yet aware that this approach was considered bad form.

The D.S. wasn't encouraging but promised to speak to the Bishop. Two weeks later he told me that the church in question had insisted on a full-time pastor, not a student. I told him I couldn't afford to stay and would have to take a secular job in Dallas. He didn't argue with me.

After the Christmas break classes resumed and a fellow student, a single man from the Nebraska Conference, said to me: "Hey, David, I just got a student appointment in Oklahoma. Maybe we can carpool." I asked him where he was assigned and he named the church in Ardmore I had sought but was told would only take a full-time pastor. My D.S. had lied to me.

So much for loyalty, good standing and the Conference caring for its own. It was the first lessons of many – systems, secular or religious, sometimes eat their young.

I took a job as a dispatcher with the Auto Impoundment Division of the Dallas Police Department. Seminary classes were in the mornings.

I went to work at 3:30 p.m. and returned home at 11:00 p.m. I studied when I could, often into the night.

The auto pound was a side of life I would otherwise never have known. I dispatched wreckers to haul in smashed or impounded vehicles which I processed into our lot, storing any personal items in the property room. When folks paid their fines, or got out of jail, I released their cars and property to them.

In time, I came to understand that all systems, including the church, are flawed. One pastor came to Annual Conference pleased his flock had asked him to return. After arriving he was told that in spite of the *official* request for his reassignment, a powerful layman in that congregation, who disliked him, had called the Bishop and insisted that the pastor be moved. The bishop acquiesced. The minister called his wife, mid-conference, and told her to start packing. They would move in less than two weeks.

He wrote a poignant lament, *Hello U-Haul, My Old Friend,* to the tune of *Sounds of Silence*. It became The Gridiron theme song for many years.

For United Methodist preachers and their families, Annual Conference was always, until recently, part business, part family reunion and always a time of renewal. We welcomed those newly ordained into our covenant fellowship, celebrated the ministry of those retiring, and stood shoulder to shoulder, bidding solemn goodbye to our departed comrades who had died that year. There was stirring preaching, from gifted visiting *leading light* preachers, to recharge our batteries. And there was time. Time with each other to strengthen the *covenant* we shared. Today, there seems to be a lack of that closeness, and Annual Conference is rushed through with less fellowship. It is a new day, not one I am pleased to see. Ah, but I am old and crochety, right?

One of the things we did was to get together with others who went to the same seminary. Such occasions brought Deans or recently published professors to speak. These were not always scintillating presentations.

One year the President of the Perkins Seminary Banquet asked my friend Rev. W. Jene Miller if he would put together a short entertainment. Jene's response was, "I will if you don't allow the Dean or a professor to speak."

Jene gathered a few of us to plan. He, Tal Oden, who was a talented musician and lawyer, and Rev. Paul Keinholtz and I began to recruit a staff, including our spouses and children for the show.

Before the days of *Laugh In,* or *That Was The Week That Was,* we wrote one-liners about funny church situations, "My treasurer told me that if I don't stop telling it like it is, the offering will never be like it was." Tal created song parodies, *O What a Beautiful Parsonage,* from *Oklahoma!* And *If I were a Bishop* from *Fiddler on the Roof.*

One-liners and skits were directed at colleagues, District Superintendents and especially the Bishop. In the first gridiron we performed a skit in which a mock Cabinet decides who is going to a particular church by throwing darts at a map of the state. Some thought it made more sense than some of the real appointments.

The banquet was a riot. While there were gales of laughter over fun poked at those who controlled our careers, those in power were not amused.

Scary, but exhilarating.

Soon the clandestine annual show became The Gridiron. In those early days no District Superintendent or Bishop came. Attendance reached several hundred each year. It provided a release of tension, and sent a not-too-subtle message to Conference leaders to use their powers judiciously. The show humanized our struggles in a system to which we had pledged our lives.

For twenty-five years I put the script together from the contributions of creative cast members. I resigned when I came into a position of leadership in the Conference and needed to "catch the barbs, not throw them."

Today, fifty plus years and counting, The Gridiron remains a popular event, no longer behind closed doors. Jene Miller, our founder, died in his late 80s. We miss his *Bunky* monologues. Until recently, the Rev. Ed Light led the group and his rendition of Garrison Keeler's Lake Woebegone, which Ed called, *Lake Bishopbegone,* was always gleefully anticipated. This year, new and younger leaders took over. Those of us who started the original group, wish the new group success on into the future.

The first bishop to attend every performance was Bishop Dan Solomon. He took the stage at the end and roasted the roasters. His best was the skit he prepared with the assistance of the Conference Communicator, Rev. Boyce Bowdon. Using a *green screen* process and shown on a large TV, we watched him in his Episcopal Robe walking on Lake Hefner, then stepping up on the dock and looking straight into the camera and saying, "Any questions?"

During his tenure Bishop Robert Hayes, Jr. sat on the front row during the show taking notes and, at the end, skewered the cast. He never made fun of the clergy or laity, only the Gridiron staff. These two Bishops are beloved because they understand that all organizations have faults.

The Gridiron continues to be a way to say to those who hurt, "We share your pain, and you are okay."

It also says to those in power, "We are watching."

If there is one thing that systems of tyranny cannot abide, it is satire.

THE EYES OF CHRISTMAS

OUR HOUSE IS QUIET ON CHRISTMAS EVE. Our kids are grown. That can't-wait glee which bubbles in children on this breath-taking evening is gone. Nobody begs to "open just one gift." Packages ring the tree, unshaken – *unpoked*.

Squeals of surprise no longer wake Paula and me at dawn on Christmas morning. We don't scramble to snap pictures as pajama clad tots search the riot of presents to see if Santa left that most hoped-for toy. Also gone is the late-night struggle to assemble those contraptions without losing every shred of one's religion or destroying the marriage.

This awe in children's eyes is unique and rarely seen in one past age twelve. How sad, for if we saw life with youthful wonderment, perhaps we would live with less stress, and more joy.

This loss of a child's perspective came home to me a few years ago. Growing up, my hometown had no swimming pool. But Ponca City, the site of the Conoco oil refinery, had a heated indoor pool for their employees and families. Occasionally outside groups could use the facilities.

The Eyes of Christmas

A trip to the refinery, especially in the winter, to swim in that wonderful pool was a treat. The building that housed this marvel rose like a palace above the bald prairie, all glassy and shiny.

Years later I attended a conference held in that refinery community. While there, my friend Neal Baumwart said he was driving out to the plant to visit his dad during lunch break. Anyone who wanted to see the place was welcome. At last – a chance to revisit this special palace of my youth.

I told him about my childhood experiences, and said it would be great to see the recreation building. He pulled into the complex, and parked in front of a low-roofed building. I said, "I'll just wait in the car, until you see your dad, and then maybe we can go see the pool."

He looked at me strangely. "This *is* the pool building!"

"Oh!" I said, "I guess they've redone it."

"No," he replied, "it's always been like this. Come in and see for yourself."

I stumbled out of the car. This could not be the palace of my childhood. Where were the great beams, the high ceilings, the wide halls? There was a pool all right, but smaller than the one I had stored in my memory. This once cavernous building was squat, dumpy and small.

But the building had not shrunk – rather my childhood sense of proportion hadn't kept up. The palace, *all glassy and shiny like a castle on the prairie* had resided only in my memory bank.

Around our house Christmas Eve is quiet. Two amazing, irrepressible children grew up. Their dancing eyes went away. For a while they brought back their own children and the experience was revived. Then the grandchildren grew up. Now great grandchildren have entered the picture. We celebrate the return of children's eyes at Christmas.

In my better moments, I don't let anything rob me of that old wonder. And upon occasion, in the quiet stillness of a yule dawn, I wake with a start, certain I heard the unmistakable squeal of children experiencing the wonder and awe of Christmas.

STANDING TALL

THE AFRICAN SUN SLIPPED BELOW THE Western horizon as our plane set down in Maputo, Mozambique. Eight of us from Oklahoma had, over the last ten days, visited United Methodist churches in Liberia, Kenya, and Zimbabwe and in three days would make an overnight stop in Johannesburg, South Africa, before returning to the United States.

Arriving hours late, the near-deserted airport was shrouded in darkness. We taxied past an ominous Russian Aeroflot, aware we were in a country whose government was friendly to Russia, not America.

In 1975, an insurgent army, Frente de Libertacao de Mocambique, or FRELIMO, was fighting for independence from Portugal. A sudden coup in Lisbon toppled the ruling party there and the victors granted Mozambique their freedom.

Two FRELIMO insurgent leaders had emerged, Eduardo Mondlane, a Christian and Samora Machel, a Marxist. During the insurgency Mondlane was killed. When independence was granted, Machel aligned the new country with the Soviets. Our group of eight met the son of Mondlane who told us, "If my father had not been killed, we would never have become a Communist country."

The new Marxist government expelled all Portuguese associated with the former regime, and Western people were advised to leave. United Methodist missionary Mary Jean Tenet refused. She defied the new government and the urging of our General Board of Missions, and stayed on through the revolution becoming beloved by the Mozambican people.

Mary Jean, who spoke excellent Portuguese, met us at the immigration booth. I presented our passports to the clerk, requesting entrance to the country. Before we left the USA, I had secured visas from every country we would visit except Mozambique. After months of trying we were told by their Embassy in Washington, D.C., "Your visas will be waiting when you arrive." Of course, they weren't.

Mary Jean spoke to the immigration clerk, then relayed to us, "He says it's irregular. No visas – no enter." The aircraft upon which we had arrived was backing away from the gate. The next plane would arrive in three days.

Mary Jean said, "The United States Charge-de-affairs' wife was on your plane. I'll see if I can catch him at the baggage claim."

She came back with a tall, slender, Yankee in tow. He was a Bostonian, representing the United States in a country where we had no embassy. He attempted to persuade the immigration officer. During the conversation our young diplomat never raised his voice.

Standing Tall

Finally, he reported to us, "Well, you may have to spend the night in the airport. The clerk has a problem. His boss has gone home for the night and he's reluctant to call him. He fears if he admits you – and wasn't supposed to – by tomorrow he'll be hanging by his thumbs. He is equally concerned that if he should let you in, and doesn't . . . he will experience the same fate. He can't make up his mind."

I assured him we'd be fine spending the night in the airport.

Our young diplomat from Boston went back and stood tall and straight in front of the booth – not uttering a word. There were no ugly-American outbursts, he made no threats or demands.

Minutes passed – then we heard the passport stamp, *kerchunk, kerchunk, kerchunk*. I wondered if that was what Teddy Roosevelt meant by: "Speak softly, and carry a big stick." We were on our way.

Silent persuasion, rolled up in a lanky New Englander, had accomplished what pleas and reason had not.

WHO IS A SIR?

THANKSGIVING WEEKEND WITH OUR California son and family ended. On Monday they returned to their pre-holiday pace. Our own busy schedules waited for us back in Oklahoma. With mixed feelings we prepared to fly home.

Arriving at the Marin air-porter bus station we were uncertain where to stand. Others around us also seemed unsure. As if in response to our anxieties, a security guard appeared. He turned to us. "Are you going to the Oakland airport?"

I responded, "Yes, sir, we are."

He straightened, turned his face to mine, and said, "*You* are the *sir*. . .I'm just the security guard." His voice was neither angry nor defensive.

My midwestern upbringing of using sir or ma'am had caught his attention. Forgetting my worry about catching the bus, I looked at him. He stood about five and a half feet tall. His Hispanic voice was soft and melodic. He peered at me through sharp, dancing eyes, his face swarthy, experience-lined.

I smiled and said, "You're a human being, aren't you?"

His grin broadened. "Yes, I am!"

"Then you are as much a *sir* as anyone, and deserve to be treated as such . . . sir."

In less time than it took the bus to turn a wide arc and park, he shared his story.

"Three weeks ago, I became a citizen of this country. I raised my hand and repeated the oath of allegiance. It took me seven long years, but I made it. They replaced my green card with a Certificate of United States Citizenship."

My mind raced. My own citizenship had never been an issue. Yet I was certain that behind his elation were multiple memories of being detained and questioned because his voice was different and his ethnic appearance categorically suspect.

"I like my job," he said. "There are many homeless people around here. I don' give them money, but sometimes I take them to the deli for a hotdog or a muffin. I try to keep an eye on 'em. The folks at the café tell me I'm crazy, but it don' hurt. I spend maybe five or six dollars a week."

Some might think he was softening me up for a big tip but I didn't think so. Over the years I've been conned, and usually comprehend the operation. The word sir had encouraged this new citizen to share himself. He now belonged to something that was bigger than all of us.

He was eager to show not only his pride, but also his sense of responsibility. His understanding of citizenship had not a hint of "I've got mine – now you get yours." As we spoke a young man came up to ask if his car was legally parked. The guard smiled and said "No. I noticed it there, but thought you'd be back in a few moments, so I didn't give you a ticket." He pointed to a lot across the street. "You can leave it there."

He turned back to me as our bus heaved into the dock. The driver stepped down and opened the luggage doors and the guard went to help load. As I brushed past him to board, I pressed a few bills in his hand. I would have given it to anyone who eased my travel, but I whispered, "God bless you."

The bus ride was an hour from Marin County to Oakland International. All airports seem to be under never-ending construction. Buses, cars, and taxis converged and spewed humanity out at a single cross-walk.

A lone security officer was directing traffic as people tried to get into the terminal and as vehicles attempted to exit. He faced formidable odds. Outbound passengers were intent on checking in. Drivers of cars were pressing to get out of the airport. It appeared this hapless officer carried the total responsibility of deciding when cars would drive and people could walk.

His only evidence of authority was a police whistle which he blew incessantly. He halted a pedestrian and forced him back to the curb. He let part of a family cross, but held back their two small children. When people walked while he was motioning a car, or autos moved when he was gesturing for people to cross – he dropped his whistle and shouted threats. He appeared to be in a state of near collapse.

Crossing at his pleasure, and standing in line to check our bags, I had a broader view. He was not, as I first thought, the only hope for order and safety. Three other uniformed officers stood at some distance, while this Lone Ranger commandeered center stage. Each time one tried to get near, the frenetic guard waved him off. Then I realized, except for our hero at traffic ground zero, who was Caucasian, the other uniformed officers were Oriental. The racist message was abundantly clear. Chaos reigned because one man thought his kind alone could perform this important task.

In the space of an hour I had witnessed two possible futures for our nation. One valued inclusiveness, the other exclusiveness.

The gentle security officer back in Marin County had modeled qualities too often lost from the fabric of our lives. Call it decency, kindness, humility, neighborliness, consideration, civility. Jesus called it love. It is, if you will, applied grace.

A PEDDLER OF HOPE

I THREATENED TO REFUSE MY PAYCHECK. Methodist preachers are responsible to see that "apportionments" are paid. These are the amounts each church sends for Annual Conference operations and world-wide missions. Pastors are not supposed to take pay if these items are not taken care of first.

One month the treasurer informed me she could not send the Conference apportionments and also pay me. The two added together were less than $1,000. I asked her how much was in the bank account.

"Well, there's about $2,800, but *I never* let the balance get below $2,500." I told her to send in the apportionments and I would tell the utilities companies and some merchants around town that we couldn't pay them because the Methodists can't afford to write us a check.

"You can't do that, she said, what will people think?"

I said, "They'll probably think the ushers ought to pass the plate again."

She paid both.

For most of my adult life I was a local church pastor of the Methodist and, after 1968, The United

Methodist Church. I pastored twelve different churches in communities with fewer than 1,500 souls to metropolitan Oklahoma City. Memberships ranged from below a hundred to over two thousand.

In 1991, Bishop Dan Solomon called and said he wanted to appoint me as the Annual Conference Director of Programming and Congregational Development. I would supervise a staff of professional lay and clergy and assist the Bishop and District Superintendents in discerning new locations for church starts. I would consult with local church leaders to improve their outreach and congregational life.

I'd do that for the next fourteen years.

The Conference staff was people with expertise in Christian Education, Campus Ministries, and Youth. Eventually it also included Camps, Volunteers in Mission and Prison Ministries. They were knowledgeable and dedicated servants. I shared with them my philosophy of management: (1. Do your job. (2. If I can help, ask. (3. Keep me informed and (4. If there is a problem, don't let me be the last to hear about it.

It worked well. I honored their skills in their respective fields, and we became an effective team. I received glowing reports from churches across the Conference, where they had visited and given leadership.

I knew little about teaching or guiding congregational development. But I learned that a new in-depth demographic analysis for communities was available, and we signed up to use its insights for our Conference. It helped congregations see their potential for new ministries. I tried to lead them to identify their strengths, opportunities and, in the process, perhaps lessen their fears of an uncertain future.

So many rural communities of our state were in free-fall. A generation or two back, their schools were full of kids, businesses on Main Street thrived, and there was incentive to grow up, stay, start a family, and prosper. But that day was evaporating like dew in the sunshine. Too many co-ops drove the local mom and pop shops out of business. Replacing old farm equipment with expensive newer machines marginalized profits. And critically, as church members aged, birth rates declined.

The reality was that children grew up and went to college because their parents wanted them to get a degree. But few came home to live and work. Their jobs were in cities far from the old home place. Then, when the folks were ready to retire and wanted to turn the farm over to a son or daughter, the kids weren't interested. Too often, the land was gobbled up by corporate farming. I soon learned that I didn't need to tell them how to develop programs copying the big city churches. What was needed was someone to lift their spirits.

Many congregations feared the day was not far off when they couldn't afford to have their own pastor or, worse, when the last few *saints* were no longer be able to keep the doors open.

Taping a sheet of newsprint on the wall I drew a circle with lines stretching from the center. In the middle I wrote the name of the congregation and asked, "Well, tell me what you are doing in your church and community." I listed their responses on the radiating lines:

"We go to the hospital and nursing homes."

I was sick and you visited me.

"We have a system of calling each other to make sure we are all okay."

This is my commandment, that you love one another, as I have loved you.

"We have a team that visits the folks in the penitentiary nearby."

I was in prison and you came to me.

"There are a few kids in our school who don't get anything to eat on the weekends, so on Fridays we provide food for their backpacks."

I was hungry and you gave me food.

"We have a community Bible School each year, and most kids in town attend.

Let the children come to me, and forbid them not.

They were deeply involved in living out Matthew's list of what it meant to serve Christ. But until they saw it on the newsprint, they hadn't realized they were still vital, fruitful and faithful.

Would they have more funerals than baptisms in a year – probably. Would they grow in members – hardly. But would they love each other from cradle to grave – absolutely.

By the time we had listed all they were doing their spirits rose. There was laughter and warmth emerging from the center of their life together.

One subject came up for which I was always prepared. It went something like this, "But we don't have babies in our church anymore. What can we do?"

I would tell them that the Annual Conference now had a new program that guaranteed babies in the nursery. "We call it the Sarah Project. It is especially created for older women in the congregation. The motto is, 'If Sarah could do it, you can too.'"

It took a few seconds before they exploded in laughter. Then I added, "Be careful, Sarah laughed and a year later she had Isaac, whose name meant '*laughter*.'"

In one church when the baby question was raised I said, "Where is your nursery?" They ushered me into a dingy space with one shaky crib and no paint on the walls. A single lightbulb hung from a cord. The bare air conditioning duct swayed across one end of the room.

I asked, "If you were a young mother, would you place your child in this nursery?"

They knew the answer. So, we talked about what parents looked for in a nursery, and suggested they were not prepared to receive a new family. We stood in a circle – held hands and I led them in prayer for what could happen in that space, and for the unknown young family that was waiting to see the brightness of a room in which they would be delighted to leave their child.

I left not knowing if anything could happen. The week after Easter, the pastor called.

"We had two babies in the nursery Easter Sunday. Please come see our new space."

Later I dropped by and rejoiced with them. The nursery walls were brightly painted; a new lower ceiling, the room amply lit, and the AC pipe covered.

Three sturdy new cribs sat on fresh carpet. It was an inviting space.

I could not reverse the inevitable shrinking of the rural population. I could not stop corporate farming from buying their beloved fields. But I could leave them with hope, affirm that they were faithful, and encourage them to continue being a loving, caring and serving congregation.

And that was all God was asking of them.

A FUNNY THING HAPPENED ON THE WAY TO RETIREMENT

I FLUNKED RETIREMENT.
The truth is, I wasn't ready.

Our church required that United Methodist clergy retire at age seventy. I reached that milestone in October of 2004, and Bishop Robert Hayes, in his first year as our bishop, said it was okay to stay until the next Annual Conference in May. It would give him time to select the next person for my job.

Early in 2005 I attended a conference in Houston designed for Conference leadership across the eight-state South Central Jurisdiction.

Some Jurisdictional leaders in Volunteers in Mission were also at that hotel. During a break several VIMers, led by Rev. Larry Norman, came to me and said, "You ought to apply for the Jurisdiction exec's position. We all think you would be the right person."

I thanked them but said that I still had a job and was planning on retirement. They countered, "Well, this isn't full time. You could do it." Their encouragement was flattering, but I thought it wasn't going to happen.

I called Paula to talk about it, but we both thought they would need someone before I'd be available. Paula, as always, was encouraging, but the timing was not right.

Flying to Dallas, after the Houston conference, to made a presentation to the College of Bishops. While there, Bishops Dan Solomon and Scott Jones and Bill Oden encouraged me to apply for the SCJ Director's vacancy.

I was warming to the idea, but knew I needed to talk to Bishop Hayes, who was not present. I flew back to Oklahoma City. As I got off the plane I heard the deep mellow voice of Bishop Hayes call out, "Hello, David." He was waiting for this plane to take him to Dallas and the College meeting. I said, "Bishop, we need to talk."

I shared my experience of the last few days and asked his opinion. He thought it a good idea, and saw no problem if I took the job a month or two before I retired.

At home I told Paula about running into the bishop. She said, "The moment I heard that the Jurisdictional position was going to be part time, I knew it was the place for you. I think you should go for it."

So, armed with the urging of the VIM leaders, two of my bishop friends, my own bishop's approval and Paula's blessing, I sent in my application.

And heard nothing.

Three weeks passed without any acknowledgement of my entry. I called the woman who was filling in after the former director had abruptly quit. Had they received my letter? Yes, but were waiting to see if others were going to apply. Not exactly heartening. The position had already been vacant several months. She said she would get back to me. *What I heard was*, "We think we can do better."

March passed and then in late April I got a call. Could I be in Dallas in May to be interviewed? *Yes, I could!*

After an interview with the search committee, they introduced me to the Mission Council as their nominee for the Director. I was elected by the Council. I started June 1, 2005, on our 50th wedding anniversary, and my last day as a full-time clergy.

Paula said, "You flunked retirement the first day."

I moved the office from Dallas to Oklahoma City. Because the former director and office manager had left suddenly, I found the financials in disarray. Bill Junk had agreed to be Jurisdictional Treasurer, but I doubt he expected to have to so quickly rescue me with his CPA skills. He is a dedicated servant of the church, and I am deeply grateful for his friendship and wisdom.

My first office manager in OKC was Mrs. Laura Patterson, whose skills were excellent and, once we had the books in order, kept them that way. When she resigned to go to work full time, I drafted Paula. She protested that she was a school teacher, not a bookkeeper, but she did well, and we worked together in joy. Of course, the first day she warned me, "One harsh word and I'm out of here."

It has been an honor, as an elected delegate to eight Jurisdictional Conferences, to have participated in the election of thirty bishops in the South Central Jurisdiction, from 1976 through 2004, and then, as Secretary, to have certified the election of the six selected since.

My responsibilities included serving as the Recording Secretary to the South Central Jurisdictional Conference sessions, and publishing the Journal of the proceedings of three conferences, Dallas, 2008, Oklahoma City, 2012 and finally Wichita in 2016.

I was honored to complete the work of Dr. Ted Agnew, who began a forty-year history of the Jurisdiction, but became too ill to complete it. Before he died he directed that his work be transmitted to my office with the request that I, along with Bishop John Wesley Hardt, finish and publish it. Bishop Hardt's sharp memory was a great help with details which only he could have supplied.

Looking back on my work life I reflected that I began my first job when I was 12 and was 82 when I retired. Work has been a delight in my life but I knew at the end of the Conference in Wichita, I was ready to give it up. If my second retirement doesn't work out – there is always the option of being a greeter at Walmart's.

I was the South Central Jurisdiction Executive Director for eleven years. I am grateful for the extension of my active time in ministry. It was a joy working with Paula. I experienced the kindness and support of the College of Bishops, and deeply appreciate the dedication of those who have served on the Mission Council. I am grateful to the Mission

Council who honored my retirement with the gift of funds for the publication of this book.

What a ride!

LETTING GO – HOLDING ON

Fewer days wait before me,
    than trail behind.
For the remaining time,
    the word is *savor!*
I will taste, breathe in,
    touch each moment.
I have nothing now
    left to prove.
No more ambitious ladders to climb
    or chutes to slide down.
I will share what I really think,
    what I truly believe.
I let go without regret,
    reach out with no apologies.
I savor the quietness with Paula,
    the serenity of her presence.
It is a time of holy holding on,
    to this I cling with joy.

MY LIFE HAS BEEN BLESSED

I WAS AN ACTIVE CLERGY, UNDER APPOINTMENT for forty-nine years, in the Oklahoma Annual Conference of the United Methodist Church. I pastored twelve churches, and served my last fourteen years on the Annual Conference staff as program director and congregational church developer. Upon retirement in 2005, I became the part-time Executive Director of the Mission Council of the South Central Jurisdiction, from which I retired in 2016. That position included serving as the recording secretary to four Jurisdictional Conferences. Including three years as a student pastor, I have served over sixty-three years.

Ministers in appointive church systems are itinerant. Some refer to it as a sent ministry. It means we agree to move as needed, appointed at the direction of a bishop. Six bishops have assigned me my place of service. Paula and I have lived in fourteen parsonages.

These stories have represented pastoral life. I hope you have found insight into human nature, and caught a glimpse of the joy of ministry.

Since 1992, Paula and I have found a spiritual home at St. Luke's United Methodist in Oklahoma City. Dr. Robert Long, the senior minister, and the staff, have welcomed us and we have been a delightful part of the Insight Sunday school class, where they allow me to teach.

Over the years I have been blessed with many colleagues. We shared the itineracy with victories celebrated and defeats endured. Their encouragement buoyed me up and their practicality calmed me down. I am grateful for the colleagueship over the years of many that will here go un-named, but especially Boyce Bowdon, Brian Bakeman, Linda Brinkworth, Fr. Paul Gallatin, John Wesley Hardt, Bill Henry, Ed Light, Bob Long, Burrell and Joann McNaught, Doug McPherson, Bill Oden, Tal Oden, Jerry Perryman, Don Johnson, Jene Miller, William I. Smith, Dan Solomon, Bonner Teeter, Mac Thompson, Jim Wheeler and David Wilson.

Of these, three couples are special to Paula and me. We travelled with Bill and Phyllis Henry, Bill and Marilyn Oden and Doug and Mary McPhersons, fished for trout, took in Mardi Gras, ate lobster in Main, visited Lincoln's Library, did jig-saw puzzles, and often talked into the night about our shared lives. It was my honor and privilege to help Bill Oden be elected as a Bishop of the church. These are dear friends whom we cherish.

I want to express my love and gratefulness to Paula who has journeyed in ministry with me for over sixty-three years and put up with me in good times and bad, continued to love me when I was less than loveable, and almost always told me my sermons were great. She has been a great pastor's wife. Together we produced two wonderful children, Sherri (married to my favorite son-in-law, John) and Art (married to my favorite daughter-in-law, Hayley) and they have blessed us with four remarkable grandchildren, who in turn now excite our lives with eight great grandchildren.

My life has been blessed.

CPSIA information can be obtained
at www.ICGtesting.com
Printed in the USA
FFHW020755161118
49448965-53787FF

9 781545 650097